TABLE OF CONTENTS

Table of contents (cont.)

Table of contents (cont.)

Introduction

By using this book you will learn the structure and usage of Standard American English.* The structure will be presented in two formats: traditional grammar terms and generative, or transformational, grammar terms. You will become self-assured with standard usage by practicing your editing skills on sentences and paragraphs.

Grammatical structure refers to the intrinsic patterns of English, which are surprisingly similar to the patterns of most other languages, and should not be confused with standard usage. According to Noam Chomsky, America's foremost linguist, ungrammatical sentences are very rarely produced by humans; not even small children produce them. An ungrammatical sentence would violate the rules of grammar, which are hard-wired into our brains. Stroke or accident victims who have sustained brain damage do sometimes produce an ungrammatical sentence, but this is because their hard-wired programs have been injured or disturbed. An example of an ungrammatical sentence is 'Bob table on bringing'. This string of words does not fit any grammatical structures in English, whether they are described in traditional or generative grammar terms.

Rules of standard usage, on the other hand, are violated every day by countless speakers of every educational, social, regional, and ethnic background. These rules have been established by academia and include the use of 'who' or 'whom', 'see' or 'seen', 'good' or 'well', 'brang' or 'brought', and the like. People who violate the rules of standard usage may do so out of ignorance or as a matter of choice. Following the rules of Standard English is not necessary one hundred per cent of the time. For example, you may want to blend into a certain social situation in which nonstandard usage is the norm. Making language choices is much like deciding what to wear. Generally you try to choose what is appropriate for the occasion. Using Standard English in some circumstances may make you feel just as awkward as wearing a suit to the beach. However, you need to have that suit in your closet when formal situations, such as academic work or a job interview, do arise. Like it or not, you are judged by your use of language.

One of the main purposes of this book is to provide you with that suit. Once you are comfortable knowing that you can follow all the rules of Standard English when the occasion calls for them, you will be able to make the appropriate choices without worry. Unfortunately, there are no tricks, no easy formulas, no shortcuts on the path to learning Standard English. The only way to be certain of the rules is to first understand the structure of English, those intrinsic patterns that you were born with the ability to comprehend. In fact, none of the material presented here is beyond the cognition of a ten-year-old, but several years of instruction have been compressed into a single volume. If you had learned grammar in tandem with reading all through the grades, you might not need this book, but chances are that this has not happened.

By learning standard English, you will become better at both reading and writing. Knowing the meaning of every word in a string does not guarantee knowing the meaning of the sentence. Meaning comes from the way in which the words are connected, and that is grammatical structure. Becoming aware of different structures and how they can be changed or moved to add subtle meaning in your own writing will definitely enhance the effect of your communication skills.

*Standard American English varies from other English dialects in some instances of spelling and comma use but not in basic grammatical structure.

i

TRADITIONAL GRAMMAR OUTLINE

I. Parts of Speech
   A. Noun - person, place, or thing
      1. common
         a. generic
         b. not capitalized
         c. boy, street, idea, etc.
      2. proper
         a. specific
         b. capitalized
         c. Todd, Park Street, Marxism, etc.
   B. Pronoun - takes the place of a noun
      1. personal (see grid on page 3)
         a. person
            (1) 1st
            (2) 2nd
            (3) 3rd
         b. number
            (1) singular
            (2) plural
         c. case
            (1) nominative (subject)
            (2) objective
            (3) possessive
      2. demonstrative
         a. points out, deictic
         b. this, that, these, those
      3. relative/interrogative
         a. connects/asks
         b. who, whom, whose, what, which, (-ever), that
   C. Verb
      1. action
         a. physical - run, put, do, etc.
         b. mental - realize, know, decide, etc.
      2. state of being
         a. forms of be - is, are, was, were, am, be, been
         b. states of growth or perception - seem, grow, become, look, smell, etc.
   D. Adjective
      1. modifies nouns
      2. tells which one, what kind of, how many
   E. Adverb
      1. modifies verbs, adjectives, and other adverbs
      2. tells when, where, why, how, to what extent, under what conditions

F. Preposition
   1. expresses adjectival or adverbial relationship between other words or phrases
   2. in, to, above, between, through, etc.
G. Conjunction
   1. coordinate
      a. connects two words, phrases, or clauses
      b. for, and, nor, but, or, yet, (and) so
   2. subordinate
      a. begins dependent clauses
      b. because, though, since, so (that), etc.
H. Article
   1. precedes nouns
   2. a, an, the

II. Elements of the Sentence
A. Form
   1. word
   2. phrase - group of related words
      a. prepositional
      b. verbal
   3. clause - group of words containing subject and predicate
      a. independent - can stand alone as a sentence
      b. dependent - cannot stand alone as a sentence
         (1) noun
            (a) whoever arrives first
            (b) that she can do it herself
         (2) adjective
            (a) which I should have known
            (b) whom we met yesterday
         (3) adverb
            (a) because it had not occurred to him
            (b) whenever we get around to it
B. Function
   1. subject - who or what does, senses, or experiences the predicate
   2. predicate (verb) - the present or past action or state of being of the subject
   3. direct object - state the subject and predicate and then ask whom or what
   4. complement - follows linking verb and is linked to the subject
      a. predicate nominative (noun)
      b. predicate adjective
   5. indirect object - state the subject and predicate and then ask to whom or what
   6. adjective - modifies nouns or other adjectives
   7. adverb - modifies verbs, adjectives, or other adverbs
   8. conjunction - connects words, phrases, or clauses

III. Types of Sentences
A. Simple - one independent clause
B. Compound - two or more independent clauses
C. Complex - one independent and one or more dependent clauses
D. Compound/Complex - two or more independent and one or more dependent clauses

Personal Pronouns, Possessive Phrases, and Relative Pronouns

Personal Pronouns are classified according to **person**, **number**, and **case**.

Person indicates whether the pronoun refers to the person speaking (1st person), the person spoken to (2nd person), or the person spoken about (3rd person).

Number indicates whether the pronoun is singular or plural.

Case indicates whether the pronoun is nominative (subject or predicate nominative) or objective (direct object, indirect object, object of preposition, or NP of infinitive).

	Nominative	Objective			*Possessive*	*Possessive Pronoun*
1st person						
singular	I	me			*my*	*mine*
plural	we	us			*our*	*ours*
2nd person						
singular	you	you			*your*	*yours*
plural	you	you			*your*	*yours*
3rd person						
singular	he, she, it	him, her, it			*his, her, its*	*his, hers, ∅*
plural	they	them			*their*	*theirs*

Examples:

Subject	**We** visited them.
Predicate Nominative	It was **they** whom we listened to.

Direct Object	He chased **her**.
Indirect Object	She gave **him** the evil-eye.
Object of Preposition	She gave the evil-eye to **you**.
NP of Infinitive	He wants **them** to leave.

Possessives and possessive pronouns are technically **NOT** personal pronouns, but their forms resemble personal pronouns in that they have person and number.

The <u>possessive form</u> can be a determiner showing possession or the NP of a gerund.

Determiner	**Their** car is old.
NP of Gerund	**My** laughing annoyed them.

The <u>possessive pronoun</u> form always takes the place of a noun.
This book is **yours**.

A <u>possessive phrase</u> is formed by adding **'s** or **'** to a noun phrase.
The **secretary's** son complained about his **sisters'** teasing.
The <u>relative pronouns</u> *who, whom, and whose* share case designations but not number or person.
Who is nominative, *whom* is objective, and *whose* is the possessive form.

Verb Forms and Tense

The **form** of a verb pertains to its morphological makeup—generally what letters have been added to the end of the root form. For example, the endings which can be added to 'walk' are -s, -ed, and -ing. 'Walks' is the third person singular present tense form (he walks); 'walked' is the past tense form for all persons and numbers (I, you, she, they walked) as well as the past participle form (they have walked); 'walking' is the present participle form (I am walking).

The **tense** of a verb is intrinsic; by definition, it is either **present** or **past**. The tense of a **verb phrase** (all of the verbs making up the predicate of a clause) is determined by the first word in the verb phrase—if that word is present tense by definition, then the whole verb phrase is present tense; if that first word is past tense by definition, then the whole verb phrase is past tense. More on tense follows the outline of verb forms.

<u>Examples</u>

Ida has been talking for an hour.
has been talking = verb phrase
has = auxiliary, present form of 'have'
been = auxiliary, past participle form of 'be'
talking = main verb, present participle form of 'talk'
tense = present perfect

Colby should have taken a nap.
should have taken = verb phrase
should = auxiliary, past modal
have = auxiliary, infinitive (and present) form of 'have'
taken = main verb, past participle form of 'take'
tense = past conditional perfect

The librarian rides her bike to school every day.
rides = verb phrase
rides = main verb, present form
tense = present

The birds are flying north.
are flying = verb phrase
are = auxiliary, present form of 'be'
flying = main verb, present participle form of 'fly'
tense = present progressive

Tim has gone home for the day.
has gone = verb phrase
has = auxiliary, present form of 'have'
gone = main verb, past participle form of 'go'
tense = present perfect

Verb Forms

I. Finite verb - leftmost verb in a verb phrase, carries tense
    <u>Can</u> be:
    A. Main verbs - rightmost verb in a verb phrase
        1. Regular
            a. past and past participle are formed by adding -ed
            b. Today I *walk*. Yesterday I *walked*. In the past I have *walked*.
        2. Irregular
            a. past and past participle have irregular forms
            b. Today I *sing*. Yesterday I *sang*. In the past I have *sung*.
        3. Copular - followed by complement (predicate noun or predicate adjective)
            a. forms of **be**
                is, are, was, were, am, be, (been, being)
            b. verbs related to the senses
                look, sound, smell, taste, feel
            c. additional copular verbs
                appear, become (get), grow, seem, remain (stay)
    B. Auxiliaries
        1. Modals

Present	Past
can	could
will	would
shall	should
may	might
must	

        2. Forms of **have**

Present	Past	Past Participle
have	had	had
has		

        3. Forms of **be**

Present	Past	Past Participle
am	was	been
is	were	
are		

        4. Forms of **do**

Present	Past	Past Participle
do	did	done
does		

II. Nonfinite verb - does <u>not</u> carry tense
    A. Verbals
        1. Infinitive
            a. form - to + verb
            b. function
                (1) noun - He wants *to win*.
                (2) adverb - He cheated *to win*.
                (3) adjective - This is the score *to beat*.
        2. Participle
            a. form
                (1) present -ing   the beat*ing* wings
                (2) past
                    (a) -ed   the roast*ed* marshmallow
                    (b) -en   the brok*en* bow
                    (c) irregular   the un*sung* hero
            b. function - adjective
        3. Gerund
            a. form
                (1) present -ing   Camping is fun.
                (2) past - X
            b. function - noun
    B. Verbs to the right of the finite (leftmost) verb in a verb phrase
        <u>Can</u> be:
        1. Main verbs   He will *go*.
        2. Auxiliaries   He will *be* going.

Three Principle Parts of a Verb

The infinitive, past tense, and past participle forms are often referred to as the **principle parts** of a verb. It is particularly important to know the principle parts of irregular verbs. Here are some examples:

<u>Infinitive</u>	<u>Past Tense</u>	<u>Past Participle</u>	
lie	lay	lain	(to repose)
lay	laid	laid	(to set down)
go	went	gone	
swim	swam	swum	
drink	drank	drunk	
sing	sang	sung	
bring	brought	brought	
come	came	come	
know	knew	known	
drive	drove	driven	
give	gave	given	
do	did	done	
think	thought	thought	

Extra Examples of Copulas

Copulas, or copular verbs, are the same as linking verbs. They denote a state of being and link the subject of the sentence to a predicate adjective or predicate noun. This section of the book is on parts of speech rather than parts of the sentence, but in some cases such as this you need to know a little bit about sentence structure in order to identify the part of speech.

A predicate adjective is an adjective that appears in the predicate half of the sentence but describes the subject. A predicate noun (predicate nominative is another term sometimes used) is a noun that appears in the predicate half of the sentence and denotes the same thing as the subject.

Here are some examples:

        PN

That boy is a little monster. 'Is' is a copula. 'Monster' is a predicate noun; it tells <u>what</u> the boy is. Remember that nouns tell what or who(m).

        PA

That boy seems really nice. 'Seems' is a copula. 'Nice' is a predicate adjective; it tells <u>what kind of</u> boy he seems to be. Remember that adjectives tell which one or what kind of.

That boy is running down the hall. There is neither a PA nor a PN here. 'Is' is an auxiliary for the main verb, 'running.'

That boy is in class. 'Is' is the main verb, but it is not a copula because 'in class' is a prepositional phrase rather than a PA or a PN. It tells <u>where</u> the boy is. Remember that prepositional phrases are either adjectival (telling which one or what kind of) or adverbial (telling when, where, why, how, to what extent, under what conditions).

        PN

The man in the gray suit is my father. 'Is' is a copula.

        PA

The dog in the back yard of the blue house sounds mean. 'Sounds' is a copula.

        PN

The dog in the back yard of the blue house is a mean one. 'Is' is a copula.

        PA

That guy smells good. 'Smells' is a copula.

That guy smells well (meaning he has sensitive olfactory nerves). 'Smells' is the main verb but not a copula. 'Well' is an adverb telling <u>how</u>.

        PA

The pizza tastes good. 'Tastes' is a copula. In order for "tastes" to be a non-copula, the subject would have to be animate and have taste buds.

Extra Examples of Participles and Gerunds

As mentioned in the extra examples of copulas, you need to know a little about sentence structure in order to identify parts of speech. Gerunds can have the exact same <u>form</u> as participles, but these two verbals will never have the same <u>function</u>. Participles will always be adjectives; gerunds will always be nouns. Another distinction between participles and gerunds is that participles often appear in both present (taking) and past (taken) forms whereas gerunds almost always appear only in their present form.

The barking dog is annoying me. 'Barking' is a participle (adjective) describing the dog. 'Annoying' is the main verb.

The barking dog is annoying. 'Barking' is still a participle, and now so is 'annoying.' They both describe the dog.

I hate that dog's barking. 'Barking' a gerund (noun); it tells <u>what</u> I hate.

Barking at strangers, our dog protects our house from intruders. 'Barking' is a participle describing 'dog'.

Barking at strangers is our dog's way of protecting our house from intruders. 'Barking' is a gerund, a noun acting as the subject of 'is'. ('Way' is a predicate noun.)

By barking at strangers, our dog protects our house from intruders. 'Barking' is a gerund; it is the object of the preposition 'by'.

Here are some more examples; the underlined words are labeled at the ends of the sentences.

The baby calf <u>crying</u> for its mother is lost.   participle
<u>Crying</u> over spilt milk will not change the situation. gerund
<u>Skiing</u> down the slope, she felt the exhilaration of freedom. participle
<u>Skiing</u> down the slope gave her a feeling of exhilaration. gerund
The women <u>eating</u> lunch together have been friends for years. participle
<u>Eating</u> lunch together is a good way to get to know your colleagues. gerund
Jasper fell asleep while <u>watching</u> television. gerund
Since <u>being</u> elected, Jason has had no time for his family. gerund
Jasmine likes <u>taking</u> tests because she is always prepared. gerund
The <u>broken</u> glass cut his feet. participle
He is <u>interested</u> in ancient history. participle (also a predicate adjective)
Those pictures <u>taken</u> at the party could be <u>incriminating</u>. both participles
The wind <u>whistling</u> down the chimney sounds eerie. participle

Verb Tenses

For reasons buried in the history of the English language, our verb forms have the possibility of exhibiting either of two tenses—PRESENT or PAST. Note that these tenses do **not** necessarily correspond to **real-world time concepts** (such as future). Remember that the leftmost verb of the verb phrase is the one that determines whether the verb phrase is PRESENT or PAST. The rest of the verb phrase may exhibit other features such as mood, aspect, and/or future time. The result is a variety of possible 'tenses' in naming the entire verb phrase. Therefore, when we name the *tense* of the leftmost verb in the verb phrase, we are speaking of tense in its particular sense—either PRESENT or PAST. When we name the 'tense' of an entire verb phrase, we are using the term more broadly, referring not only to its tense but its mood, aspect, and possibly time reference as well. When a verb phrase contains a finite verb, the phrase has 'tense' and is called a **predicate**.

A main verb can be expanded in eight ways (tense markers PRESENT and PAST in the examples are arbitrary):

1. tense + verb   (PAST + walk = walked)
2. tense + modal + verb   (PRES + modal + walk = will walk)
3. tense + perfect + verb   (PRES + perfect + walk = has walked)
4. tense + progressive + verb   (PAST + progressive + walk = was walking)
5. tense + modal + perfect + verb
              (PAST + modal + perfect + walk = would have walked)
6. tense + modal + progressive + verb
              (PRES + modal + progressive + verb = will be walking)
7. tense + perfect + progressive + verb
              (PAST + perfect + progressive + verb = had been walking)
8. tense + modal + perfect + progressive + verb
       (PRES + modal + perfect + progressive + verb = will have been walking)

Modal auxiliaries indicate **conditional** mood; conditional mood indicates possibility.
He may go.   He might go.   He can go.   He could go.   He would go.   He should go.

Because modals are related to possibility, they sometimes indicate **future time**.
He will go.   He shall go.

Aspect indicates whether the action of the verb is completed or continuing; aspect occurs in two varieties—perfect and progressive. **Perfect** aspect shows that the action of a verb is completed and is indicated by an auxiliary form of 'have' plus the past participle form of the verb. **Progressive** aspect shows that the action of a verb is continuing, or 'in progress', and is indicated by an auxiliary form of 'be' plus the present participle (-ing) form of the verb.

The twenty possible predicate tenses of the verb 'to begin' are listed below:

1. present perfect

have (has) begun

2. present conditional perfect progressive

may (can) have been beginning

3. past conditional perfect progressive

would (could, should, might, must) have been beginning

4. past perfect (pluperfect)

had begun

5. present progressive

is (am, are) beginning

6. future

will (shall) begin

7. present conditional progressive

can (may) be beginning

8. past perfect progressive

had been beginning

9. past conditional progressive

would (could, should, might, must) be beginning

10. present conditional

can (may) begin

11. future perfect

will (shall) have begun

12. past conditional

would (could, should, might, must) begin

13. present

begin(s)

14. past progressive

was (were) beginning

15. future perfect progressive

will (shall) have been beginning

16. past

began

17. future progressive

will (shall) be beginning

18. present conditional perfect

may (can) have begun

19. present perfect progressive

have (has) been beginning

20. past conditional perfect

would (could, should, might, must) have begun

Active, Passive, and Middle Voice

Voice refers to the relationship between structural grammar and role relations. Common terms involving structural grammar are subject, object and prepositional phrase. Role relations have more to do with semantics, or the meaning of a sentence. In its simplest form, the concept of role relations determines who did what to whom and under what sorts of conditions. For example, 1) 'the dog chased the cat' renders the same semantic meaning as 2) 'the cat was chased by the dog,' but the two sentences have different structural patterns. In both sentences, the semantic role of the dog is that of <u>agent</u>, and the semantic role of the cat is that of <u>patient</u>; however, structurally, the subject in sentence 1) is 'dog' whereas the subject of sentence 2) is 'cat'. We refer to 1) as having active voice because the semantic agent is the structural subject of the sentence and 2) as having passive voice because the semantic patient is the subject of the sentence while the agent becomes the object of the preposition 'by'. When the prepositional phrase is deleted, we are left with 3) 'the cat was chased'; this sentence, though structurally complete, has lost the semantic role of agent.

A predicate is in **active voice** when the grammatical subject of the sentence is also the functional agent (doer) of the predicate.

<u>Example</u>
Amy shut the door.

A predicate is in the **passive voice** when the grammatical subject of the sentence is the functional patient (receiver) of the predicate. If the agent is in the sentence, it is the object of the preposition 'by'. Passive voice is created by a form of 'be' + past participle form of the verb.

<u>Examples</u>
The door was shut by Amy.
The door was shut.

Some languages have a grammatical representation for **middle voice**, in which there is no agent or patient of the predicate.

<u>Example</u>
The door shut.

Practice with Verb Forms and Tense

For each sentence fill in the blanks with the appropriate verb forms and tell what the tense of the entire verb phrase is. Copular verbs will appear in both the copula and main verb blanks. Modals will appear in both the modal and auxiliary blanks.

EXAMPLE: Bill had been thinking about going to Iowa, but he changed his mind.

Verb Phrase   Verbals

modal _____   participle _____

copula _____   gerund going_____

auxiliary had, been_____   infinitive _____

main verb ____thinking___/ changed

tense _had been thinking - past perfect progressive _/ changed - past_

1. The underlying reason for his illness was that he would not allow himself time to eat healthy meals.

Verb Phrase   Verbals

modal _____   participle _____
copula _____   gerund _____
auxiliary _____   infinitive _____
main verb _____

tense _____

2. Since they have left us this money, we can go to the store and buy food.

Verb Phrase   Verbals

modal _____   participle _____
copula _____   gerund _____
auxiliary _____   infinitive _____
main verb _____

tense _____

3. They will have been studying for three hours by the time they finish this review.

Verb Phrase   Verbals

modal _____   participle _____
copula _____   gerund _____
auxiliary _____   infinitive _____
main verb _____

tense _____

4. Teresa is becoming a beautiful young lady, and her striking features attract a lot of attention.

Verb Phrase   Verbals

modal _____   participle _____
copula _____   gerund _____
auxiliary _____   infinitive _____
main verb _____

tense _____

5. A barking dog has been causing the neighbors to call the police and complain.

Verb Phrase   Verbals

modal _____   participle _____
copula _____   gerund _____
auxiliary _____   infinitive _____
main verb _____

tense _____

6. After they had bought the supplies for the party, several of the guests told them that they weren't coming.

Verb Phrase   Verbals

modal _____   participle _____
copula _____   gerund _____
auxiliary _____   infinitive _____
main verb _____

tense _____

7. She will be the perfect bride; her eyes are brimming with tears, and the ceremony hasn't even started yet.

Verb Phrase   Verbals

modal _____   participle _____
copula _____   gerund _____
auxiliary _____   infinitive _____
main verb _____

tense _____

8. Audrey has been listening to the radio to see if it will snow.

Verb Phrase   Verbals

modal _____   participle _____
copula _____   gerund _____
auxiliary _____   infinitive _____
main verb _____

tense _____

9. I wonder if the car will start this morning or if I will need a tow.

Verb Phrase   Verbals

modal _____   participle _____
copula _____   gerund _____
auxiliary _____   infinitive _____
main verb _____

tense _____

10. Teams that like practicing usually win more games.

Verb Phrase   Verbals

modal _____   participle _____
copula _____   gerund _____
auxiliary _____   infinitive _____
main verb _____

tense _____

11. Whenever Tom has thrown a ball into the shrubbery, his dog has retrieved it.

Verb Phrase   Verbals

modal _____   participle _____
copula _____   gerund _____
auxiliary _____   infinitive _____
main verb _____

tense _____

12. Having realized her mistake, Jami decided to change her course of action.

Verb Phrase   Verbals

modal _____   participle _____
copula _____   gerund _____
auxiliary _____   infinitive _____
main verb _____

tense _____

13. The smell of baked chicken was beginning to lure the dinner guests toward the kitchen.

Verb Phrase   Verbals

modal _____   participle _____
copula _____   gerund _____
auxiliary _____   infinitive _____
main verb _____

tense _____

14. Jake might have won the race if his leg had not developed a cramp and caused him to slow his pace.

Verb Phrase   Verbals

modal _____   participle _____
copula _____   gerund _____
auxiliary _____   infinitive _____
main verb _____

tense _____

Key to Practice with Verb Forms

1. The underlying reason for his illness was that he would not allow himself time to eat healthy meals.

Verb Phrase   Verbals

modal ____would____   participle __underlying__

copula ____was____   gerund _____

auxiliary ____would____   infinitive __to eat__

main verb __was, allow__

tense __was – past / would allow – past conditional__

2. Since they have left us this money, we can go to the store and buy food.

Verb Phrase   Verbals

modal ____can____   participle _____
copula _____   gerund _____
auxiliary ____have, can____   infinitive _____
main verb ____left, go and buy____

tense __have left – present perfect / can go and buy – present conditional__

3. They will have been studying for three hours by the time they finish this review.

Verb Phrase   Verbals

modal ___will___   participle _____
copula _____   gerund _____
auxiliary __will, have, been__   infinitive _____
main verb __studying, finish__

tense will have been studying – future perfect progressive / finish - present

4. Teresa is becoming a beautiful young lady, and her striking features attract a lot of attention.

Verb Phrase   Verbals

modal _____   participle ____striking_____
copula ____becoming_____   gerund _____
auxiliary __is_____   infinitive _____
main verb __becoming, attract_____

tense ____is becoming – present progressive / attract - present_____

5. A barking dog has been causing the neighbors to call the police and complain.

Verb Phrase   Verbals

modal _____   participle ___barking_____
copula _____   gerund _____
auxiliary ____has, been_____   infinitive __to call and (to) complain__
main verb ____causing_____

tense ____has been causing – present perfect progressive_____

6. After they had bought the supplies for the party, several of the guests told them that they weren't coming.

Verb Phrase   Verbals

modal _____   participle _____
copula _____   gerund _____
auxiliary _had, were(n't)_____   infinitive _____
main verb __bought, told, coming_____

tense _had bought – past perfect / told – past / were(n't) coming – past progressive_____

7. She will be the perfect bride; her eyes are brimming with tears, and the ceremony hasn't even started yet.

Verb Phrase   Verbals

modal __will_____   participle _____
copula __be_____   gerund _____
auxiliary __will, are, has(n't)_____   infinitive _____
main verb _be, brimming, started_____

tense will be – future / are brimming – present progressive / has(n't) started – present perfect

8. Audrey has been listening to the radio to see if it will snow.

Verb Phrase   Verbals

modal ____will_____   participle _____
copula _____   gerund _____
auxiliary __has, been, will_____   infinitive ___to see_____
main verb _listening, snow_____

tense ___has been listening – present perfect progressive / will snow – future

9. I wonder if the car will start this morning or if I will need a tow.

Verb Phrase   Verbals

modal ____will, will_____   participle _____
copula _____   gerund _____
auxiliary __will, will_____   infinitive _____
main verb _wonder, start, need_____

tense _wonder – present / will start – future / will need – future

10. Teams that like practicing usually win more games.

Verb Phrase   Verbals

modal _____   participle _____
copula _____   gerund __practicing_____
auxiliary _____   infinitive _____
main verb _like, win_____

tense ____like – present / win - present_____

11. Whenever Tom has thrown a ball into the shrubbery, his dog has retrieved it.

Verb Phrase   Verbals

modal _____   participle _____
copula _____   gerund _____
auxiliary _has, has_____   infinitive _____
main verb __thrown, retrieved_____

tense __has thrown – present perfect / has retrieved – present perfect____

12. Having realized her mistake, Jami decided to change her course of action.

Verb Phrase   Verbals

modal _____   participle ___(having) realized_____
copula _____   gerund _____
auxiliary ___having_____   infinitive _to change_____
main verb ____decided_____

tense __decided – past_____

13. The smell of baked chicken was beginning to lure the dinner guests toward the kitchen.

Verb Phrase   Verbals

modal _____   participle ___baked_____
copula _____   gerund _____
auxiliary ___was_____   infinitive ___to lure_____
main verb _beginning_____

tense ____was beginning – past progressive_____

14. Jake might have won the race if his leg had not developed a cramp and caused him to slow his pace.

Verb Phrase   Verbals

modal ___might_____   participle _____
copula _____   gerund _____
auxiliary _might, have, had_____   infinitive _to slow_____ _____
main verb _won, developed and caused__

tense _might have won – past conditional perfect / had developed and caused - past perfect

Coordinating and Subordinating Conjunctions

Coordinating conjunctions join two or more equal structures—words, phrases, or clauses. They are *and, or, nor, but, for, so,* and *yet.*

Examples:
The meal was expensive *but* good. (joining two adjectives)
Andrew drove his car around the corner *and* into a light post. (joining two prepositional phrases)
The swim team practiced diligently, *yet* it placed fifth in the meet. (joining two clauses)

Subordinating conjunctions introduce dependent (subordinate) clauses, which act as adjectives, adverbs, or nouns.

Subordinating conjunctions that introduce clauses acting as adjectives are called relative pronouns, and the clauses are called **relative clauses**. They tell which one or what kind of:

who	which	where
that	whose	why
whom		when

Subordinating conjunctions that introduce clauses acting as adverbs are simply called subordinating conjunctions, and the clauses are called **adverb clauses**. They tell when, where, why, how, to what extent, or under what conditions:

after	before	unless
although	if	until
as	in order that	when
as if	since	whenever
as long as	so that	where
as though	than	wherever
because	though	while

Subordinating conjunctions that introduce clauses acting as nouns are also simply called subordinating conjunctions, but the clauses are called **complement clauses**. They tell who or what:

whoever	if
whomever	where
whosever	when
what	whether
whatever	why
that	how
whom	
who	

PRACTICE TEST ON PARTS OF SPEECH #1

Apply the directions below to all of the following sentences. It is important that you **follow the directions in order** and that you **list the words in the order** in which they appear in the sentences.

1. While the ants were dragging their food into the little holes in the sand, the grasshoppers began to think about preparing for the long winter.

2. Stella had been a nightclub singer before she married the man of her dreams; now they have two children and a lovely house in the suburbs.

3. Conner would have become awfully lonesome on his twentieth birthday if you had not mentioned the idea of going to see a live radio show.

4. Toni has been catching mice in the cardboard houses with sticky floors, but Jan prefers to kill them instantly with the original type of trap that people bait with cheese or peanut butter.

A. List all **articles** here and then cross them out of the sentences.

1. _____

2. _____

3. _____

4. _____

B. List all **modals** here and then cross them out of the sentences.

1. _____

2. _____

3. _____

4. _____

C. List all **copulas** here and then cross them out of the sentences.

1. _____

2. _____

3. _____

4. _____

D. List all **auxiliaries** here and then cross them out of the sentences.

1. _____

2. _____

3. _____

4. _____

E. List all **main verbs** here and then cross them out of the sentences.

1. _____

2. _____

3. _____

4. _____

F. List all **participle modifiers** here and then cross them out of the sentences.

1. _____

2. _____

3. _____

4. _____

G. List all **gerunds** here and then cross them out of the sentences.

1. _____

2. _____

3. _____

4. _____

H. List all **infinitives** here and then cross them out of the sentences.

1. _____

2. _____

3. _____

4. _____

I. List all **prepositions** here and then cross them out of the sentences.

1. _____

2. _____

3. _____

4. _____

J. List all **nouns** here and then cross them out of the sentences.

1. _____

2. _____

3. _____

4. _____

K. List all **personal pronouns** here and then cross them out of the sentences.

1. _____

2. _____

3. _____

4. _____

L. List all **possessives** here and then cross them out of the sentences.

1. _____

2. _____

3. _____

4. _____

M. List all **possessive pronouns** here and then cross them out of the sentences.

1. _____

2. _____

3. _____

4. _____

N. List all **possessive phrases** here and then cross them out of the sentences.

1. _____

2. _____

3. _____

4. _____

O. List all **demonstratives** here and then cross them out of the sentences.

1. _____

2. _____

3. _____

4. _____

P. List all **attributive adjectives** here and then cross them out of the sentences.

1. _____

2. _____

3. _____

4. _____

Q. List all **predicate adjectives** here and then cross them out of the sentences.

1. _____

2. _____

3. _____

4. _____

R. List all **adverbs** here and then cross them out of the sentences.

1. _____

2. _____

3. _____

4. _____

S. List all **coordinating conjunctions** here and then cross them out of the sentences.

1. _____

2. _____

3. _____

4. _____

T. List all **subordinating conjunctions** here and then cross them out of the sentences.

1. _____

2. _____

3. _____

4. _____

Write the entire verb phrase of each clause and tell which of the twenty tenses it is.

1. _____

_____

2. _____

_____

_____

3. _____

_____

4. _____

_____

_____

KEY TO PRACTICE PARTS OF SPEECH TEST #1

A.
    1. the, the, the, the, the
    2. a, the, a, the
    3. the, a
    4. the, the

B.
    3. would

C.
    2. been
    3. become

D.
    1. were
    2. had
    3. have, had
    4. has, been

E.
    1. dragging, began
    2. married, have
    3. mentioned
    4. catching, prefers, bait

G.
    1. preparing
    3. going

H.
    1. to think
    3. to see
    4. to kill

I.
    1. into, in, about, for
    2. of, in
    3. on, of
    4. in, with, with, of, with

J.
    1. ants, food, holes, sand, grasshoppers, winter
    2. Stella, singer, man, dreams, children, house, suburbs
    3. Conner, birthday, idea, show
    4. Toni, mice, houses, floors, Jan, type, trap, people, cheese, butter

K.
    2. she, they
    3. you
    4. them

L.
    1. their
    2. her
    3. his

P.
    1. little, long
    2. nightclub, two, lovely
    3. twentieth, live, radio
    4. cardboard, sticky, original, peanut

Q.
    3. lonesome

R.
    2. now
    3. awfully, not
    4. instantly

S.
    2. and
    4. but, or

T.
    1. while
    2. before
    3. if
    4. that

1. were dragging – past progressive
    began – past
2. had been - past perfect (pluperfect)
    married – past
    have – present
3. would have become – past conditional perfect
    had mentioned – past perfect (pluperfect)
4. has been catching – present perfect progressive
    prefers – present
    bait – present

PRACTICE PARTS OF SPEECH PRACTICE TEST #2

Apply the directions below to all of the following sentences. It is important that you **follow the directions in order** and that you **list the words in the order** in which they appear in the sentences.

1. Walking to her dorm room, the biology major decided that she hadn't had enough chemistry to do well in her cell biology course.

2. The biggest problem with having a double major is trying to get into the necessary courses within five years.

3. As a fifth year student, he had been able to register for classes before the other students registered.

4. Education majors spend a large amount of time observing other teachers, who build up the profession.

5. If you have ever looked carefully at a book after judging it by its cover, you will have realized that this is the reason for the proverb.

A. List all **articles** here and then cross them out of the sentences.

1. _____

2. _____

3. _____

4. _____

5. _____

B. List all **modals** here and then cross them out of the sentences.

1. _____

2. _____

3. _____

4. _____

5. _____

C. List all **copulas** here and then cross them out of the sentences.

1. _____

2. _____

3. _____

4. _____

5. _____

D. List all **auxiliaries** here and then cross them out of the sentences.

1. _____

2. _____

3. _____

4. _____

5. _____

E. List all **main verbs** here and then cross them out of the sentences.

1. _____

2. _____

3. _____

4. _____

5. _____

F. List all **participles** here and then cross them out of the sentences.

1. _____

2. _____

3. _____

4. _____

5. _____

G. List all **gerunds** here and then cross them out of the sentences.

1. _____

2. _____

3. _____

4. _____

5. _____

H. List all **infinitives** here and then cross them out of the sentences.

1. _____

2. _____

3. _____

4. _____

5. _____

I. List all **prepositions** here and then cross them out of the sentences.

1. _____

2. _____

3. _____

4. _____

5. _____

J. List all **personal pronouns** here and then cross them out of the sentences.

1. _____

2. _____

3. _____

4. _____

5. _____

K. List all **nouns** here and then cross them out of the sentences.

1. _____

2. _____

3. _____

4. _____

5. _____

L. List all **possessives** here and then cross them out of the sentences.

1. _____

2. _____

3. _____

4. _____

5. _____

M. List all **possessive pronouns** here and then cross them out of the sentences.

1. _____

2. _____

3. _____

4. _____

5. _____

N. List all **possessive phrases** here and then cross them out of the sentences.

1. _____

2. _____

3. _____

4. _____

5. _____

O. List all **demonstratives** here and then cross them out of the sentences.

1. _____

2. _____

3. _____

4. _____

5. _____

P. List all **attributive adjectives** here and then cross them out of the sentences.

1. _____

2. _____

3. _____

4. _____

5. _____

Q. List all **predicate adjectives** here and then cross them out of the sentences.

1. _____

2. _____

3. _____

4. _____

5. _____

R. List all **adverbs** here and then cross them out of the sentences.

1. _____

2. _____

3. _____

4. _____

5. _____

S. List all **coordinating conjunctions** here and then cross them out of the sentences.

1. _____

2. _____

3. _____

4. _____

5. _____

T. List all of the **subordinating conjunctions** and then cross them out of the sentences.

1. _____

2. _____

3. _____

4. _____

5. _____

Write the entire verb phrase of each clause and tell which of the twenty tenses it is.

1. _____

_____

2. _____

3. _____

_____

4. _____

_____

5. _____

_____

_____

KEY TO PRACTICE PARTS OF SPEECH TEST #2

A.
    1.the
    2. the, a, the
    3. a, the
    4. a, the
    5. a, the, the

B.
    5. will

C.
    2. is
    3. been
    5. is

D.
    1. hadn't
    3. had
    5. have, have

E.
    1. decided, had
    3. registered
    4. spend, build
    5. looked, realized

F.
    1. Walking
    4. observing

G.
    2. having, trying
    5. judging

H.
    1. to do
    2. to get
    3. to register

I.
    1. to, in
    2. with, into, within
    3. as, for
    4. of
    *up is a particle or an adverb; it does not have an object and therefore cannot be a preposition
    5. at, after, by, for

J.
    1. she
    3. he
    5. you, it, you

K.
    1. room, major, chemistry, course
    2. problem, major, courses, years
    3. student, classes, students
    4. majors, amount, time, teachers, profession
    5. book, cover, reason, proverb

L.

    1. her, her
    5. its

O.

    5. this

P.

    1. dorm, biology, enough, cell, biology
    2. biggest, double, necessary, five
    3. fifth, year, other
    4. Education, large, other

Q.

    3. able

R.

    1. well
    4. up
    5. ever, carefully

T.

    1. that
    3. before
    4. who
    5. If, that

1.   decided – past
       hadn't had – past perfect (pluperfect)

2.   is – present

3.   had been – past perfect (pluperfect)
       registered – past

4.   spend – present
       build – present

5.   have looked – present perfect
       will have realized – future perfect
       is – present

TRADITIONAL AND TRANSFORMATIONAL GRAMMARS

Grammar is the study of structural relationships in a language, i.e. how words and their component parts combine to form sentences. **Traditional grammar** in English developed several centuries ago in the British Isles when English became more than just the vernacular of the people and began to be taught in the schools. Until then, the languages of educated people were Latin and Greek, both highly regularized languages with rather complicated grammars. When educated Englishmen decided to establish grammatical rules for English in order to raise its status as a scholarly language, they simply adopted the same structural categories that they had learned in Latin and forced English into the slots so easily occupied by Latin.

Because English is not even in the same language family as Latin (English is Germanic; Latin is a Romance language), there arose several problems with trying to impose the structure of one language upon the usage of another. For this reason, traditional grammar has many "exceptions to the rule," a situation which may have contributed to its lack of popularity in the modern school curriculum. In the mid-20th century, however, a young linguistics scholar named Noam Chomsky began working on an entirely different approach to the structure of English which led to a much more feasible way of dealing with English grammar.

The major difference between traditional grammar's approach to structure and Chomsky's approach is that the former is **prescriptive** while the latter is **descriptive**. In other words, traditional grammar had a set of rules adopted from Latin, and the use of those rules was prescribed. If your use of language did not follow the rules, you were WRONG. Chomsky, on the other hand, realized that if a one- or two-year-old could understand and use language, then there must be an internal structure to it that is recognizable by the human brain. Therefore he set out to learn and describe the intrinsic rules of English and to compare these patterns, which we innately follow, with patterns of other languages. These patterns that are similar in all languages he called **universals**. Chomsky's descriptive approach to grammar was earlier referred to as **generative** but is now more often called **transformational**.

In this book you will learn both approaches—traditional and transformational. Remember that it is the same structure you are looking at. It simply has two perspectives and two sets of vocabulary. Thus far, you have learned the traditional terminology for **parts of speech**. In transformational grammar they are called **categories.** Next you will learn how **elements of the sentence** form sentences (for the traditional outline, refer back to pp. 1-2). In transformational grammar terms, you will be learning **phrase structure rules**.

Traditional Grammar Main Sentence Elements

Phrase = group of related words
        Ex: noun phrase – the scruffy ruffian
          verb phrase – had been walking stealthily
          prepositional phrase – into the night
Clause = group of words having a subject and a predicate
        Ex: She sells seashells.   although the Cubs won

Sentence = a group of words which must contain at least one independent clause
        Ex: She sells seashells.

Independent clause = clause which expresses a complete thought
        Ex: She sells seashells.

Dependent clause = subordinate clause = clause which functions as an adjective, adverb, or noun
        Ex: although the Cubs won

Subject = the noun (who or what) that does the action or experiences the state of the predicate
        Ex: although the Cubs won
        Ex: Alfie is sick.

Predicate = the action or state of being done or experienced by the subject
        Ex: although the Cubs won
        Ex: Alfie is sick.

Direct object = the noun (whom or what) that receives the action of the verb
                d.o.
        Ex: Corrine likes apples.

Indirect object = the noun (whom or what) that receives the object of a verb related semantically
        to 'give'   i.o.   d.o.
        Ex: Corrine sent her mother a basket of apples.

Predicate noun = noun (who or what) following a copular verb and meaning the same thing as
        the subject   p.n.
        Ex: Ronnie is a fireman.

Predicate adjective = adjective following a copular verb and describing the subject
             p.a.
        Ex: Ronnie is brave.

Prepositional Phrase = preposition plus a noun phrase, which is the object of the preposition
        prep. object of prep. (o.p.)
        Ex. in the garden

Transformational Grammar Sentence Elements

S = sentence (NP + VP)

NP = noun phrase*   N = noun

VP = verb phrase   V = verb

AP = adjective phrase   A = adjective

AdvP = adverb phrase   Adv = adverb

PP = prepositional phrase   P = preposition

Conj = conjunction (compound structures)

Det = determiner (this includes articles, possessives, and demonstratives)

*The term "phrase" in transformational grammar is different from its traditional grammar meaning.

Transformational Grammar Phrase Structure Rules

If a sentence element has (parentheses) around it, that means the element is optional: it may be in the structure, but it is not necessary. Notice that all phrases must contain a **head** (N is the head of NP, V is the head of VP, etc).

S → NP VP   A sentence <u>must</u> contain a noun phrase and a verb phrase.

NP → (Det) (AP) N (PP) A noun phrase <u>may</u> contain a determiner, adjective phrase, and/or prepositional phrase; it <u>must</u> contain a noun.

VP → (AdvP) (aux) (neg) V (NP) (PP)

AP → (AdvP) (AP) A (PP)

AdvP → (AdvP) Adv (PP)

PP → P NP Note that a prepositional phrase <u>must</u> contain a preposition (the head) <u>and</u> a noun phrase (in traditional terms, the object of the preposition).

Conj → α conj α   Ex: NP conj NP, VP conj VP, PP conj PP, etc. The alpha symbol stands for any like structures.

Parsing and Treeing

Now that you understand the two sets of terminology for individual words in a sentence, you are ready to learn how to analyze the structure of a sentence and see how those words relate to one another. When we analyze a sentence in traditional grammar, we **parse** it. The instructions for parsing are below. Parsing is done on a linear level. When we analyze a sentence in transformational grammar, we **tree** it. Trees are hierarchical in structure. It does not matter what phrases are next to one another in a tree, but it does matter what phrases are above and below one another. This is because traditional grammar is concerned with the **surface structure** of a sentence, the way the word order appears as it is spoken or written. Transformational grammar, on the other hand, is concerned with the **underlying, or deep, structure** of a sentence, the structure of the sentence before any transformations are made to bring it to its present surface structure. In the next pages you will learn how first to parse a sentence and see how the parts of its surface structure relate to one another. Then you will learn how to tree a sentence and see how the parts of its underlying structure relate to one another. If your curiosity about how the two methods of analysis look side by side is overwhelming, you may look ahead to sample sentences on page 48 before returning to the parsing and treeing instructions.

Parsing Instructions

Underline all simple **subjects once** and simple **predicates twice**.

Put brackets around subordinate clauses and label them **R** for relative, **C** for complement, and **A** for adverb.

Put parentheses around phrases and label them **PP** for preposition, **inf** for infinitive, **ger** for gerund, **part** for participle, and **app** for appositive.

Draw solid arrows from all modifiers to the words they modify, including phrase modifiers and clause modifiers.

Put **d.o.** over direct objects, **i.o.** over indirect objects, **p.a.** over predicate adjectives, and **p.n.** over predicate nouns.

Draw dotted arrows from direct objects to their corresponding verbs, including verbals.

Parsing Sentences: Dotted and Solid Arrows

When parsing the surface structure of sentences, draw a **dotted arrow** from the direct object to the verb that governs it. A direct object must be a noun or pronoun. It tells whom or what. To find the direct object, say the subject of the sentence; then say the verb; then ask whom or what? The answer will be the direct object. The main verb in the predicate *governs* the direct object.

Tami baked a cake.

d.o.

Tami <u>baked</u> a cake.   Tami baked what? A cake.   Cake is the direct object.

d.o.

<u>Theresa won</u> a silver medal for her performance of a Vivaldi concerto.

Theresa won what? A medal. Medal is the direct object.

When parsing the surface structure of sentences, draw a **solid arrow** from any modifiers to the words that they modify. Modifiers are either adjectives or adverbs (refer to D and E on page 1 in the traditional grammar outline). They can be one-word modifiers, such as *blue* or *lightly*, they can be multi-word modifiers, such as *bright royal blue* or *very tricky*, or they can be phrases, such as *in the window* or *of my name*. When drawing a solid arrow, you do not need to tell whether it is an adjective or an adverb. You just need to connect it to the word that it modifies.

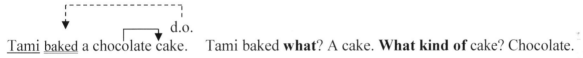

d.o.

<u>Tami baked</u> a chocolate cake.   Tami baked **what**? A cake. **What kind of** cake? Chocolate.

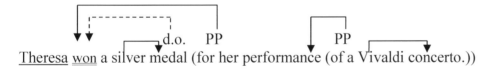

d.o.   PP   PP

<u>Theresa won</u> a silver medal (for her performance (of a Vivaldi concerto.))

Theresa won **what**? A medal. **What kind of** (or **which**) medal? Silver. **Why** did she win it? For her performance. **What kind of** (or **which**) performance? Of a concerto. **What kind of** concerto? A Vivaldi one. You know that *silver*, *Vivaldi*, and *of a Vivaldi concerto* are all adjectives because they tell **which one** or **what kind of**. And they point to nouns because that's what adjectives modify (adjectives can also modify other adjectives but not in this sentence). *For her performance* tells **why** Theresa won the medal, so that makes it an adverb. Therefore it points to a verb. (Adverbs can also modify adjectives and other adverbs but not in this sentence.) Notice that *for her performance of a Vivaldi concerto* **contains** *of a Vivaldi concerto* rather than being separate from it. This is because *of a Vivaldi concerto* modifies a word inside of the first PP and so is **part** of that first PP. Parsing and treeing sentences will make you a better reader.

Parsing Sentences: Predicate Adjectives and Predicate Nouns

Predicate adjectives are treated just like any other adjectives in parsed sentences. They point to the word that they modify with a solid arrow. The word that they modify will always be the subject of the sentence or clause (in simple sentences there will be only one clause, and that is the sentence).

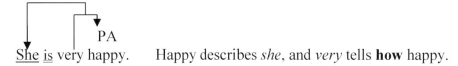

She is very happy.   Happy describes *she*, and *very* tells **how** happy.

If you drew the arrow pointing to *she* directly from the word *happy* rather than from *very happy*, you would not be wrong.

Predicate nouns are very similar to direct objects in surface structure (parsing) and exactly like direct objects in underlying structure (treeing). They both answer the question who(m) or what after you say the subject and the predicate. However, in surface structure, a predicate noun (PN) follows a copula while a direct object follows a transitive verb. A copula denotes a state of being whereas a transitive verb denotes an action. A predicate noun denotes the same entity as the subject, and the direct object receives the action of the verb.

                          PN
Chuck became the president of the archery club last year.

                          d.o.
Chuck married the president of the archery club last year.

The reason we draw arrows from direct objects to their verbs but do not draw arrows from predicate nouns is that, as you will see when we get into more complex sentences, there may be several verbs in a sentence; and the dotted arrow is needed to connect the direct object to the verb that governs it. In the case of predicate nouns, on the other hand, they must denote the same entity as the subject that they are linked to by the copular verb. Consequently, there is no need for an arrow because the predicate noun is necessarily bound to its subject.

Here is an example of a sentence in which it is not obvious which verbs govern which direct objects. Before long you will be parsing and treeing sentences such as this but not quite yet.

He is neglecting studying for class and spending time with his friends.

We know that he is neglecting studying for class; however, is he also neglecting spending time with his friends, or is he spending time with his friends instead of studying for class? Parsing and treeing sentences will make you a better writer.

Using Phrase Structure Rules and Making Trees

Always refer to the phrase structure rules on page 40 when first beginning to tree sentences. Remember that these are descriptive, not prescriptive, rules. They simply describe the language structures that are already programmed in your brain. What you are doing now is becoming conscious of them. After you practice treeing sentences for a while, your neural paths will know where to take you, and you will no longer have to think of the rules consciously.

The grammatical structures on the right side of the arrow tell you that they are possible **constituents** of the grammatical structure on the left side of the arrow. That means that in a tree these grammatical structures on the right side of the arrow can appear below the **node** of the grammatical structure on the left side of the arrow. Soon you will see the relationships between the abstract sentence structures represented by the transformational trees and the surface structures represented by parsing in traditional grammar. For example, the phrase structure rules of transformational grammar say that an S must have an NP and a VP. This would be the same as saying in traditional terms that a sentence must have a subject and a predicate.

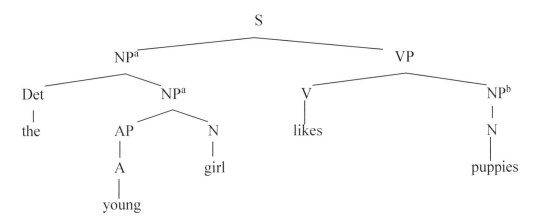

A **constituent** is a node which has at least two **branches** below it plus everything that is below that node. Therefore, the top NP^a, the Det, the second level NP^a, the AP, the N, and the A all make up a constituent. The second level NP^a, the AP, the N, and the A also make up a constituent. The VP, V, NP^b, and N make up a constituent; but the AP and A do not make up a constituent, and neither do the NP^b and N because the AP and the NP^b have only one branch, which leads to their respective heads. When you make trees, you will not be labeling the different NPs and VPs with superscript a's and b's. This is done here only to identify and distinguish them from one another. Other terms involving constituents are **mother, daughter,** and **sister**. The AP (young) and N (girl) are sisters of one another and daughters of NP^a, which is their mother.

You will notice that each node has no more than two branches coming from it. This is an arbitrary rule which many linguists subscribe to in order to show the precise hierarchical relationships between grammatical structures. You may see a textbook which illustrates three or more branches coming from a node. It simply means that this textbook is demonstrating sentence trees in a more general fashion and that the book probably includes other aspects of linguistics besides just syntax.

Carrying a Phrase Down to Lower Levels in the Tree

The previous page explained that we will limit the number of branches coming from a node to two or one. Here is another way of thinking about a type of phrase which is carried down to lower levels.

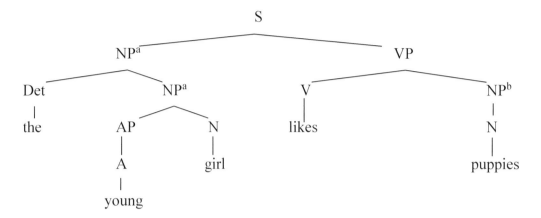

In this tree, think of the two NP^as as being the exact same phrase. It only appears this way in order to satisfy our agreement to limit the number of branches coming from a single node. If we did not, the constituent could look like this, but we will not use this method.

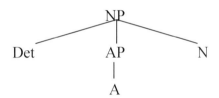

Another way to think of these nodes being carried down is like this:

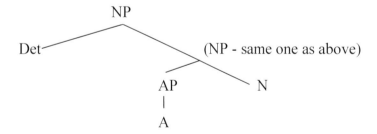

Here the NP that is labeled "same one as above" is another way of showing that the two NP^as are the same as in the tree at the top of the page.

Treeing a VP Containing More Than One Other Phrase

On the pages entitled "Using Phrase Structure Rules and Making Trees" and "Carrying a Phrase Down to Lower Levels in a Tree," you saw that the reason a phrase may be carried down to a lower level is to preserve our agreement to limit the number of branches coming from a single node to two or one. As you tree more sentences, you will notice that VPs typically have a lot of branches coming from them. Look back at the phrase structure rules, and you will see why. There are more possible grammatical structures to be contained in a VP constituent than in other grammatical structures.

It is important that you understand this concept because a tree may have more than one configuration and still illustrate an accurate analysis of a sentence. The keys provided for the practice sentences show only one configuration. Your tree may look different and still be correct. If you understand this concept, you will know whether your trees are correct or not even when they do not match the keys exactly.

Because a VP may contain one or two NPs (direct and indirect objects), any number of adverbs, and any number of prepositional phrases, it has the possibility of having lots of branches coming from it. (In parsing this will be reflected by all of the arrows pointing to the main verb.) Here is a sample of the variety of ways in which the same VP may be illustrated:

Alan happily gave Aunt Gloria a ride on Sunday after church.

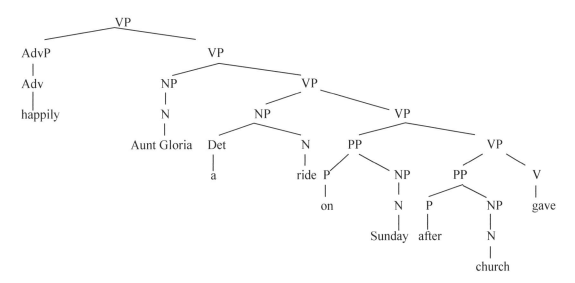

The phrases 'happily,' 'Aunt Gloria,' 'a ride,' 'on Sunday,' and 'after church' all come from the VP. It does not matter in what order they appear. All that matters is that the V, the head of the VP, is not listed above any of the other phrases that come off the VP (it is above the N church, but the PP, not the N, comes off the VP, and the V is not above the PP). Following are some alternative configurations for this VP. There are many more.

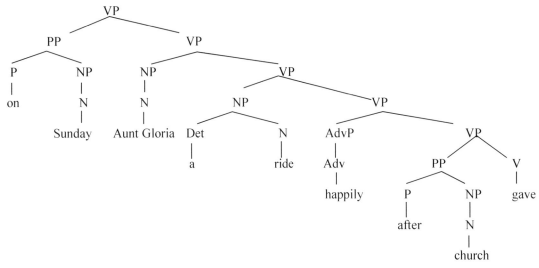

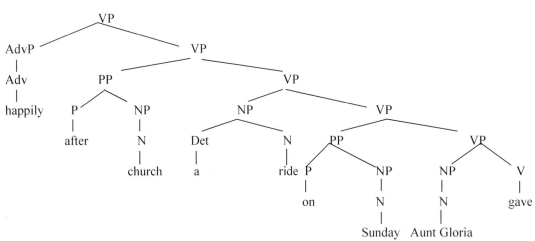

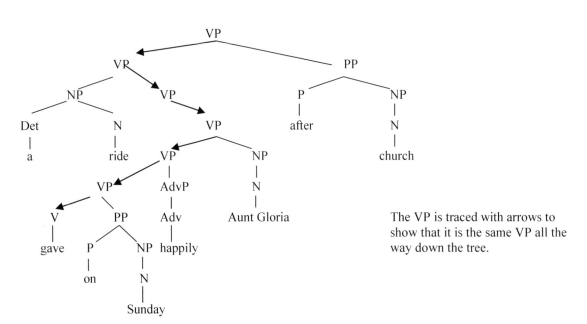

The VP is traced with arrows to show that it is the same VP all the way down the tree.

Sample Sentences Parsed and Treed

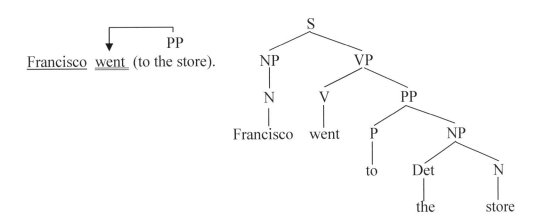

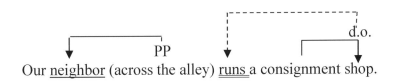

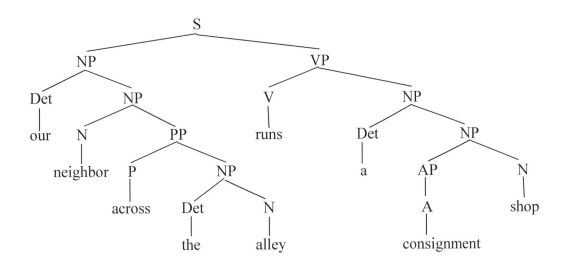

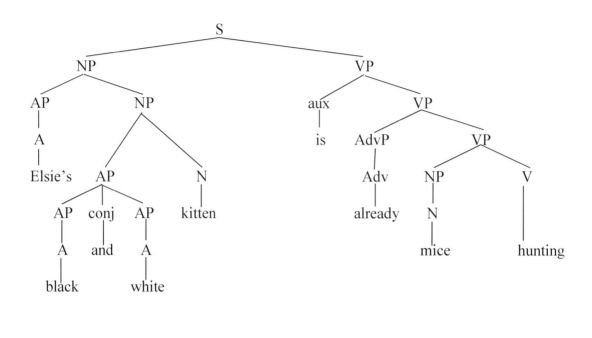

Elsie's black and white <u>kitten</u> <u>is</u> already <u>hunting</u> mice.

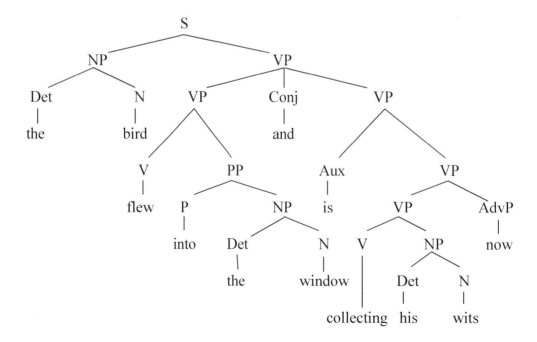

The <u>bird</u> <u>flew</u> (into the window) and <u>is</u> now <u>collecting</u> his wits.

Practice Parsing and Treeing #1

1. Our chicken clucks at strangers.

2. The majority of the students went to the party.

3. Most of Juan's socks were in the dryer.

4. In the beginning was the word.

5. The calendar always has pretty pictures on it.

6. Sometimes criminals feel remorse for their crimes.

7. The whisper of wind through the pines told Abigail a love story.

8. Predicate adjectives modify the subject of the sentence.

9. Tony is blue.

10. Grammar trees are great fun.

Practice Parsing and Treeing #2

1. The little puppies romped and tugged at one another's tails.

2. Orange and purple clothes violate the dress code.

3. Charelle's mother and Tookie's sister have been best friends for years.

4. Under the table you will find a small child and her pet snake.

5. Dillon mowed the lawn on Monday and weeded the garden on Tuesday.

6. The accountant was tired, but he finished his work by midnight.

7. Until yesterday I had not started my assignments for biology or speech.

Key to Practice Parsing and Treeing #1

1. Our <u>chicken</u> <u>clucks</u> (at strangers).   The object of the preposition, *strangers*, is not labeled because the noun following a preposition is always the o.p. Possessives are not adjectives.

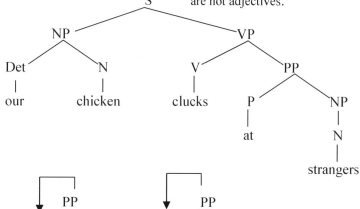

2. The <u>majority</u> (of the students) <u>went</u> (to the party).   Notice that PPs can be either adjectival or adverbial, depending on whether they modify a noun or a verb, but they are simply labeled as PPs, not A or Adv.

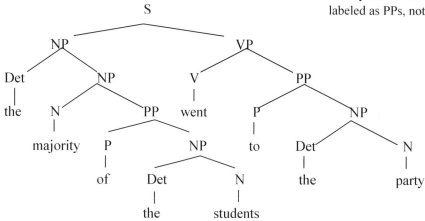

3. <u>Most</u> (of Juan's socks) <u>were</u> (in the dryer).

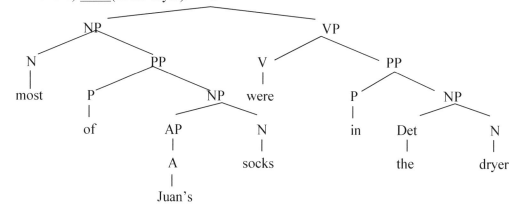

51

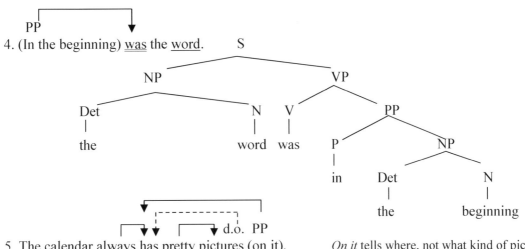

4. (In the beginning) was the word.

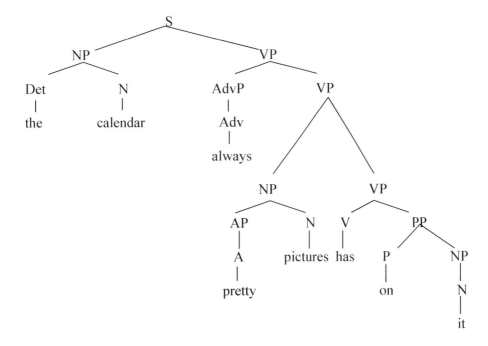

5. The calendar always has pretty pictures (on it).   *On it* tells where, not what kind of pictures.

The AdvP, NP, and PP coming off of the VP are all pointing to the verb *has* in the linear sentence, so that means they must all come off of the VP. But in the tree they can all change positions with one another. Because trees are hierarchical, it does not matter which comes off first, second, or third. It only matters that the V is on the lowest level. See pages 46-47. Think of all the VPs as just the continuation of one VP.

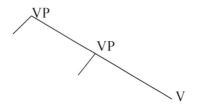

6. Sometimes <u>criminals</u> <u>feel</u> remorse (for their crimes).

Remember to ask yourself the functional questions when determining modifiers and direct objects (pp. 1-2). Criminals feel *what*? Remorse. *What kind of* remorse? Remorse for their crimes. *When* do they feel it? Sometimes.

```
                        S
            _____/ _____
          NP                         VP
          |                   _____/ _____
          N                  VP                NP
          |              ___/ \___          ___/ \___
       criminals      AdvP       V        PP          N
                       |         |      _/ \_      remorse
                      Adv       feel   P     NP
                       |         |     |    _/ \_
                   sometimes    for   Det    N
                                       |     |
                                     their  crimes
```

7. The <u>whisper</u> (of wind (through the pines)) <u>told</u> Abigail a love story.

We do not need to draw an arrow from the indirect object to the verb because it will always be the object of the same verb that governs the direct object.

```
                               S
                   _____/ _____
                 NP                           VP
          _____/ _____              _____/ _____
        Det            NP            NP               VP
         |         ___/ \___         |          _____/ \_____
        the       PP        NP       N        NP             V
               __/ \__      |     Abigail   _/ \_          told
              P      NP     N            Det    NP
              |    __/ \__  |             |    _/ \_
              of  PP      N whisper       a   AP     N
                _/ \_     |                    |    story
               P    NP   wind                  A
               |   _/ \_                        |
            through Det  N                     love
                    |    |
                   the  pines
```

Through the pines tells what kind of wind. Therefore it comes off of the same NP node as *wind* in the tree; in the linear parsing the *through the pines* PP points to *wind*, and the ending parentheses include one PP within the other.

53

8. Predicate <u>adjectives</u> <u>modify</u> the subject (of the sentence).

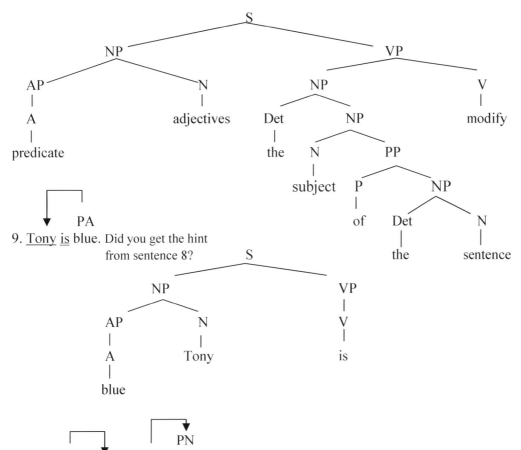

9. <u>Tony</u> <u>is</u> blue. Did you get the hint from sentence 8?

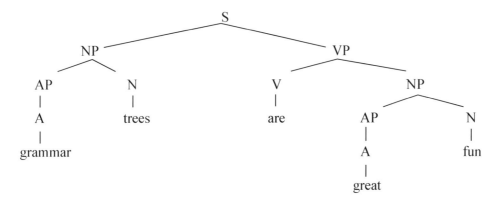

10. Grammar <u>trees</u> <u>are</u> great fun. Did you have trouble deciding whether *fun* was a predicate adjective or a predicate noun? *Fun* is usually a noun though it is used colloquially as an adjective, as in *we had a fun time*. The certain evidence, however, that *fun* is a noun rather than an adjective is that its modifier is *great*, which is an adjective. If *fun* were an adjective, its modifier would have to be the adverb form, *greatly*.

Notice that PNs look no different from d.o.s once they get into the tree.

Key to Practice Parsing and Treeing #2

When you analyze sentences with conjoined structures, make sure that you understand exactly which structures are being conjoined and which structures modify the parts of the conjoined structures.

1. The little <u>puppies</u> <u>romped and tugged</u> (at one another's tails). The puppies did not romp at one another's tails.

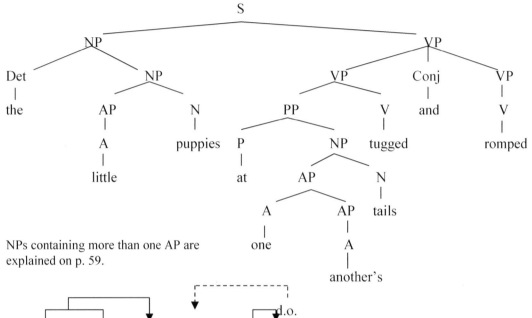

NPs containing more than one AP are explained on p. 59.

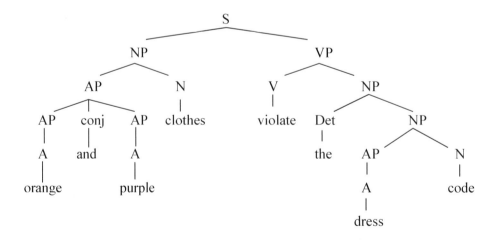

2. Orange and purple <u>clothes</u> <u>violate</u> the dress code.

55

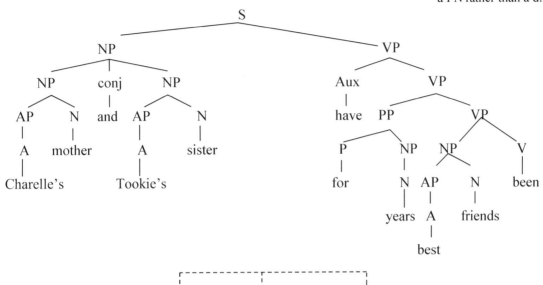

3. Charelle's <u>mother</u> and Tookie's <u>sister</u> <u>have been</u> best friends (for years). Remember that *been* is a copular verb, so it gets a PN rather than a d.o.

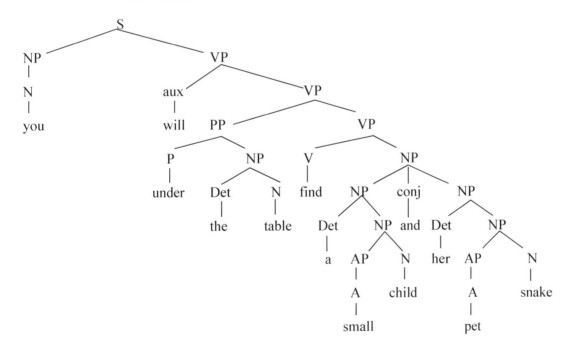

4. (Under the table) <u>you</u> <u>will find</u> a small child and her pet snake.

56

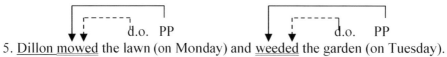

5. <u>Dillon mowed</u> the lawn (on Monday) and <u>weeded</u> the garden (on Tuesday).

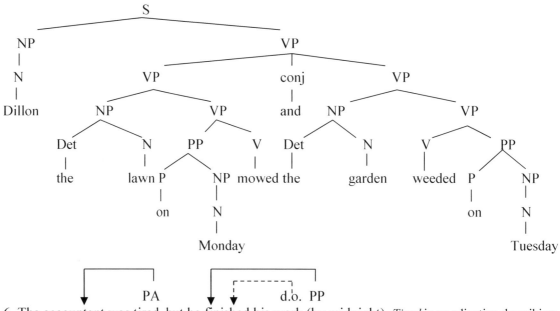

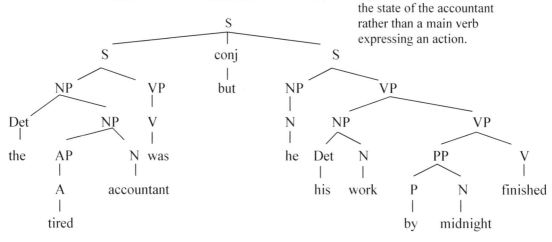

6. The <u>accountant was</u> tired, but <u>he finished</u> his work (by midnight). *Tired* is an adjective describing the state of the accountant rather than a main verb expressing an action.

57

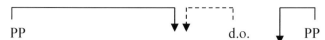

7. (Until yesterday) I had not started my assignments (for biology or speech).

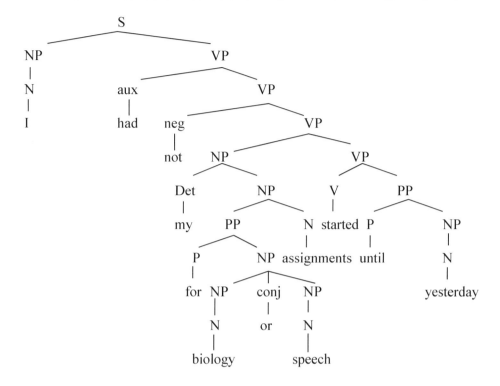

Not can be treated as an adverb in linear parsing or simply left alone. In the tree it gets its true label, negative.

NPs Containing More Than One Adjective

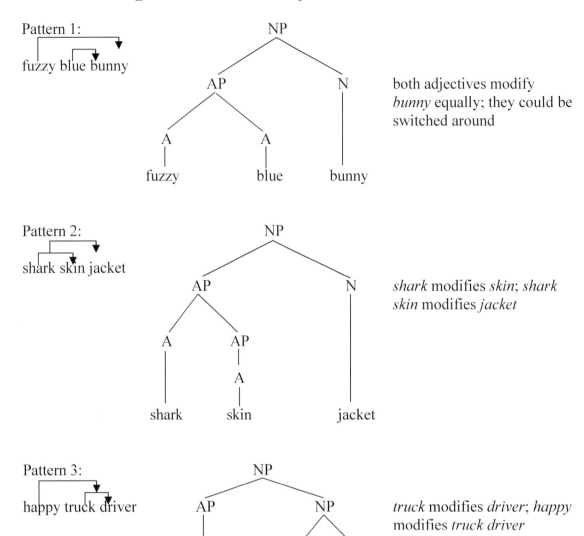

Pattern 1:

fuzzy blue bunny

both adjectives modify *bunny* equally; they could be switched around

Pattern 2:

shark skin jacket

shark modifies *skin*; *shark skin* modifies *jacket*

Pattern 3:

happy truck driver

truck modifies *driver*; *happy* modifies *truck driver*

Practice Parsing and Treeing #3

1. The fuzzy white rabbit bounced away from its owner.

2. The strict art teacher graded his students on attendance.

3. All of the third year students took the Victorian novel course.

4. The Columbian government's head honcho fell into the hands of the drug lords.

Key to Practice Parsing and Treeing #3

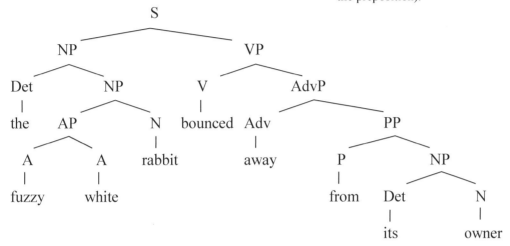

1. The fuzzy white <u>rabbit</u> <u>bounced</u> away (from its owner). *Away* is not a preposition because it does not have an object. Remember that according to the phrase structure rules a PP <u>must</u> contain a P and an NP (the object of the preposition).

```
                        S
              ┌─────────┴─────────┐
             NP                   VP
          ┌───┴───┐           ┌───┴───┐
         Det      NP          V       AdvP
          |     ┌──┴──┐       |     ┌──┴────┐
         the   AP     N    bounced Adv      PP
             ┌──┴──┐   |           |      ┌──┴──┐
            A      A  rabbit      away    P     NP
            |      |                      |   ┌──┴──┐
          fuzzy  white                   from Det    N
                                              |      |
                                             its    owner
```

2. The strict art <u>teacher</u> <u>graded</u> his students (on attendance). Notice that the NP pattern with two adjectives is different from that in sentence 1.

```
                           S
                ┌──────────┴──────────┐
               NP                     VP
          ┌─────┴─────┐          ┌────┴────┐
         Det          NP        NP         VP
          |        ┌───┴───┐  ┌──┴──┐    ┌──┴──┐
         the      AP       NP Det    N   V      PP
                  |      ┌──┴──┐ |    |   |   ┌──┴──┐
                  A     AP    N his students graded P    NP
                  |     |     |                    |     |
                strict  A   teacher               on     N
                        |                                |
                       art                          attendance
```

60

3. <u>All</u> (of the third year students) <u>took</u> the Victorian novel course.

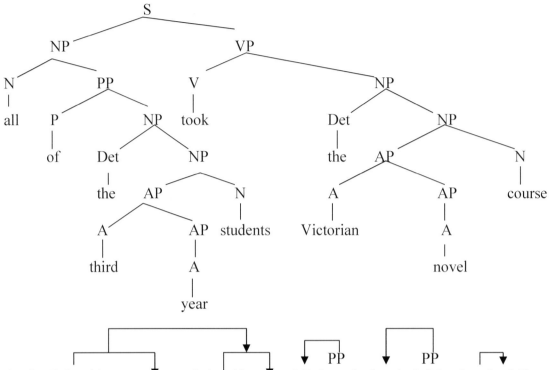

4. The Columbian government's head <u>honcho</u> <u>fell</u> (into the hands (of the drug lords)).

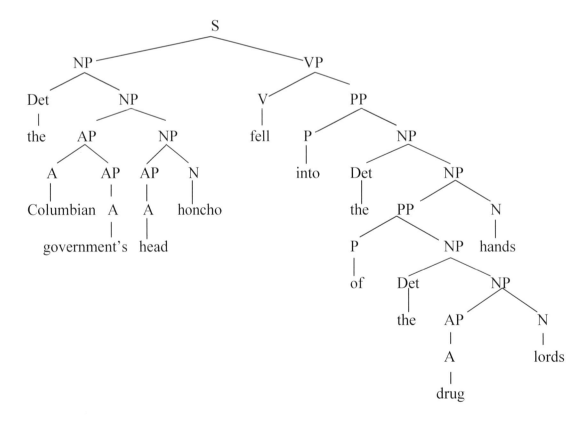

Ambiguity in Surface Structure

Prepositional phrases, adjective phrases, and conjoined constituents can create ambiguity in surface structure. That is, the sentence can be understood to have more than one meaning. However, each meaning will have a different underlying structure.

Example with PP: The devil tempted the woman with an apple.

Meaning 1: The devil tempted a woman who had an apple.
Meaning 2: The devil used an apple to tempt the woman.

Tree for meaning 1:

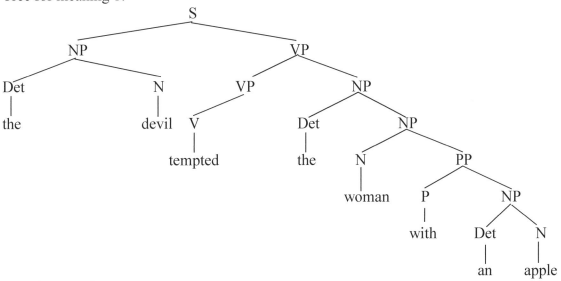

Tree for meaning 2:

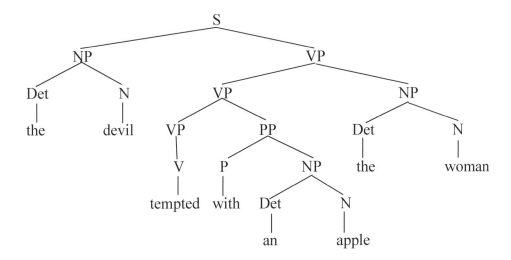

Example with AP: He is an old car driver.

Meaning 1: He drives an old car.
Meaning 2: He is old and drives a car.

Tree for meaning 1:

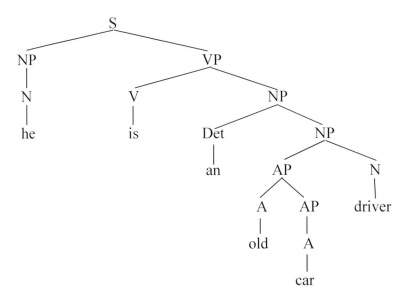

Tree for meaning 2:

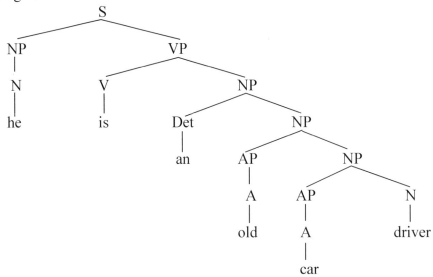

Example with Conj: I like green eggs and ham.

Meaning 1: I like ham and green eggs.
Meaning 2: I like green eggs and green ham.

Tree for meaning 1:

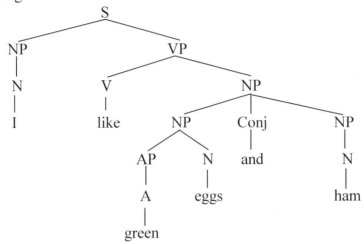

Tree for meaning 2:

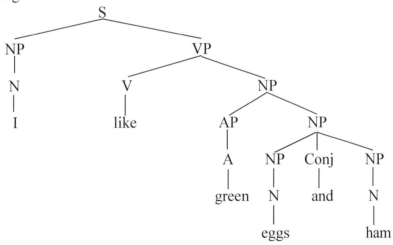

Practice Parsing and Treeing Ambiguous Sentences

1. Dan gave his phone number to the girl in the pickup. (2 trees)

2. The little boy hid the present from his uncle. (2 trees)

3. Cappy brought flowers to the old woman on his paper route. (2 trees)

4. The mugger hit the old gentleman with a cane. (2 trees)

5. The French history teacher tested his students every Friday. (2 trees)

6. The attractive young women and men sang Christmas carols in the mall. (3 trees)

7. Everyone complained about difficult assignments and schedules. (2 trees)

Key to Practice Parsing and Treeing Ambiguous Sentences

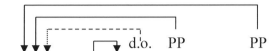

1a. <u>Dan gave</u> his phone number (to the girl) (in the pickup). This tells where Dave was when he
gave the girl his number; it does not tell
where the girl was.

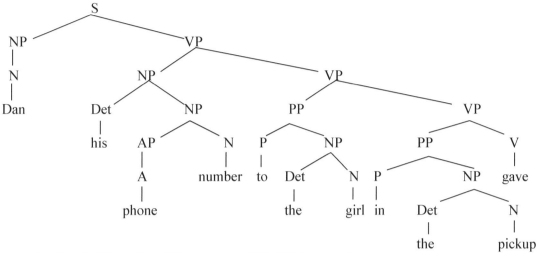

Remember that the NP and both PPs can come off the VP in any order,
but the V must be on the last level to ensure that each VP has a V in it.

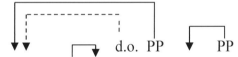

1b. <u>Dan gave</u> his phone number (to the girl (in the pickup)). This tells which girl Dave gave
his number to, the one in the pickup.

The missing parts of the trees remain the same in the *b* and *c* sentences.

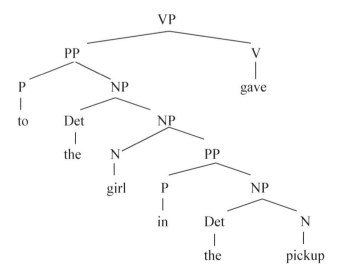

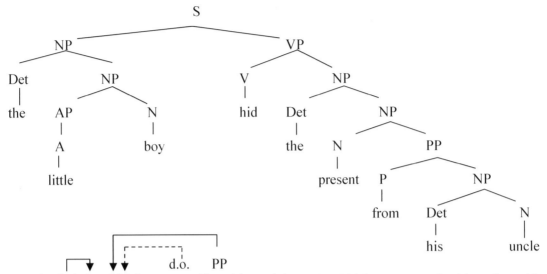

2a. The little <u>boy</u> <u>hid</u> the present (from his uncle). This tells which present the boy hid.

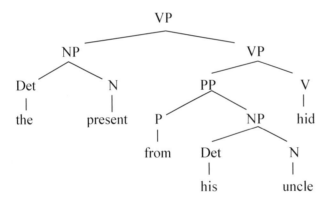

2b. The little <u>boy</u> <u>hid</u> the present (from his uncle). The boy hid the present so that his uncle could not find it.

3a. <u>Cappy</u> <u>brought</u> flowers (to the old woman) (on his paper route). This tells when Cappy brought flowers to the old woman— while he was on his paper route.

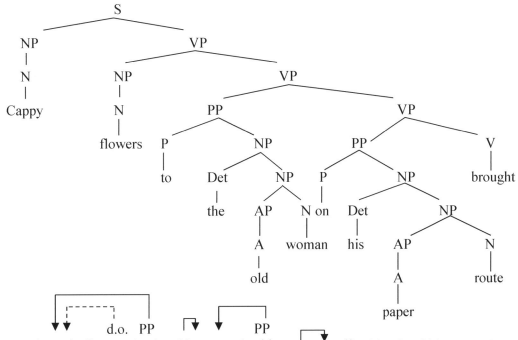

3b. <u>Cappy</u> <u>brought</u> flowers (to the old woman (on his paper route)). This tells which woman Cappy brought flowers to--the one on his paper route.

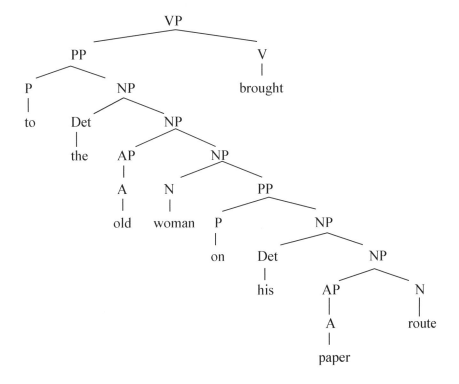

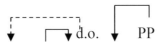

4a. The <u>mugger</u> <u>hit</u> the old gentleman (with a cane). The old gentleman had a cane.

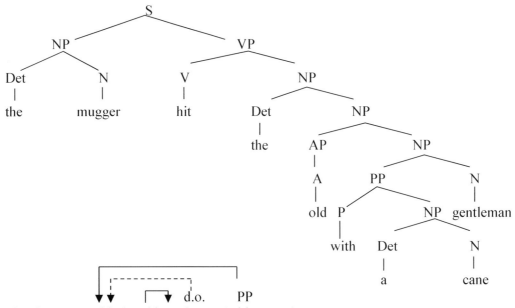

4b. The <u>mugger</u> <u>hit</u> the old gentleman (with a cane). The mugger used a cane to hit the old gentleman.

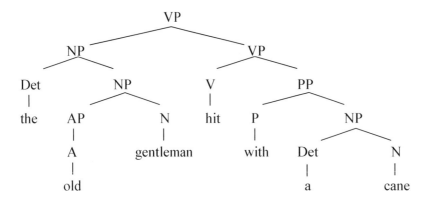

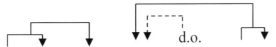

5a. The French history <u>teacher</u> <u>tested</u> his students every Friday. *Friday* is called an adverbial noun in traditional grammar because it is a thing (noun) that tells when (adverb). The arrow from it to *tested* treats it as an adverb, and the arrow from the adjective *every* to *Friday* treats it as a noun.

The teacher teaches French history.

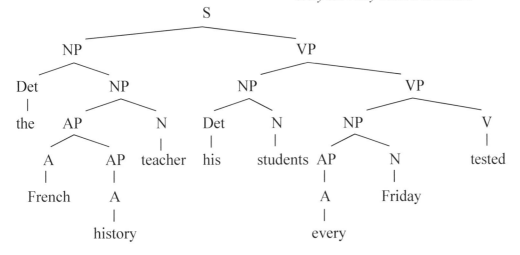

In transformational grammar there is no need to conjure terms for *every Friday*; the tree simply follows the phrase structure rules.

5b. The French history <u>teacher</u> <u>tested</u> his students every Friday. The history teacher is from France.

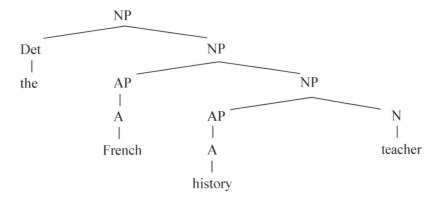

6a. The attractive young <u>women</u> and <u>men</u> <u>sang</u> Christmas carols (in the mall). The women and men are all both attractive and young.

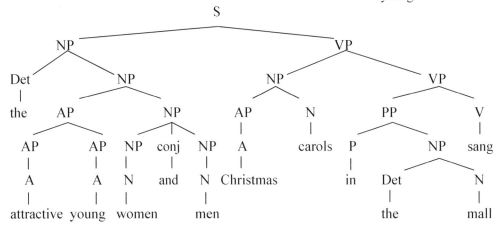

6b. The attractive young <u>women</u> and <u>men</u> <u>sang</u> Christmas carols (in the mall). The women and men are both attractive, but only the women are young.

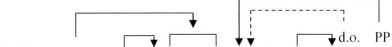

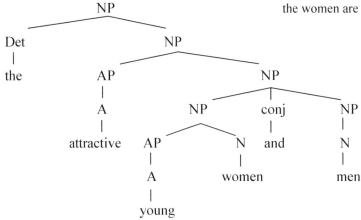

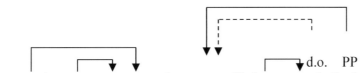

6c. The attractive young <u>women</u> and <u>men</u> <u>sang</u> Christmas carols (in the mall). Only the women are
attractive and young.

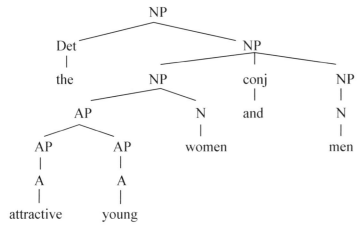

7a. <u>Everyone</u> <u>complained</u> (about difficult assignments and schedules). Both the assignments and schedules are difficult.

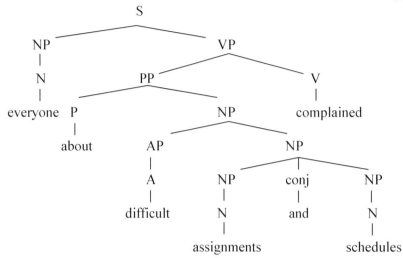

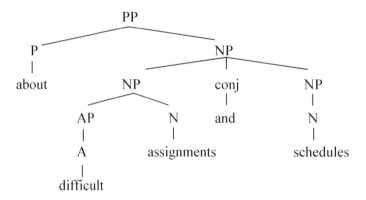

7b. <u>Everyone</u> <u>complained</u> (about difficult assignments and schedules). Only the assignments are difficult.

Clauses

Review the structure of clauses on your traditional grammar outline and the subordinating conjunctions that introduce them on page 20. One of the surface structure 'rules' for English is that a subordinating conjunction must introduce a subordinate clause. In underlying structure, however, that conjunction may not have originated in subject NP position. To show the relationship between underlying and surface structure, we will start adding a COMP position to the trees. This is a place to which we move a subordinating conjunction in order to show where it came from in underlying structure and where it moved to in surface structure. This move is called a **transformation**, thus the term 'transformational grammar'. If the subordinating conjunction is the subject of the clause, it will already be in initial position and will not need to move into COMP. In this case, COMP will remain empty with a null sign. You must understand the underlying structure of the clause in order to identify the case of the subordinating conjunction. In your own writing, this means that you will be able to correctly choose when to use 'who' and 'whom'.

In the sentences below, the italicized adjectives, adverbs, and nouns in the first set can be replaced with the adjective, adverb, and noun clauses in the second set. Notice that in the case of adjectives, single-word adjectives are prepositioned in surface structure; adjective clauses, on the other hand, are postpositioned.

On the next page, the sample sentence is first parsed and treed with a single-word noun; then the matching noun clause is parsed and treed. Following that page the sentence is parsed and treed with the clause in order to show the transformation from underlying to surface structure; that is, it shows the movement of the subordinating conjunction. Practice parsing and treeing clauses with the rest of the sentences. They are parsed and treed for you beginning on page 77.

1. We will give candy to *him*.
2. Tristan can play *later*.
3. The *gold* necklace was expensive.
4. They opened the presents *early*.
5. They like *everyone*.
6. We *understandably* headed for shelter.
7. The *little* sweater is very warm.
8. *Handsome* Jack Colby loves horses.

1. whoever comes to the door
2. when he is finished with his homework
3. that John gave his girlfriend for her birthday
4. after the guests had arrived
5. whomever they met at George's party on Saturday
6. since the tornado was fast approaching the trailer park
7. which Sandy knitted for her neighbor's dog
8. who became one of the most famous hog ropers in history

Sample sentence with single word NP (cookies):

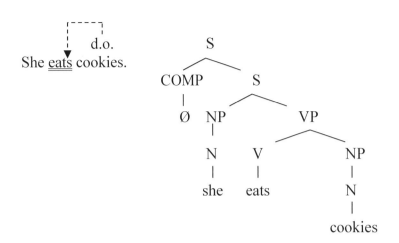

Sample complement (noun) clause:

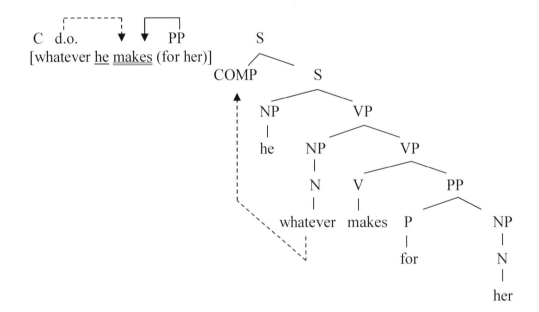

The dotted line represents the transformation which occurs between underlying and surface structure. This graphic may help you picture the process:

- surface structure

- transformation (movement required to satisfy surface structure 'rules')

- underlying structure

Surface structure 'rules' account for most language differences in grammar. Underlying structure reveals the universality of language.

Sample sentence with noun clause:

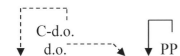

She eats [whatever he makes (for her)]. The word *whatever* is the direct object of the verb *makes*.
The entire complement clause is the direct object of the verb *eats*.

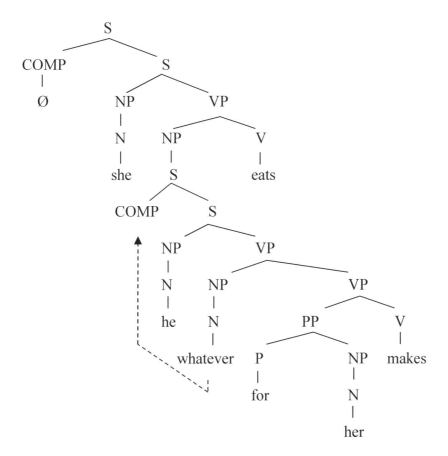

The subordinate clause S fits into the sentence in the same way it does for any other adjective, adverb, or noun phrase. Simply bring a line straight down from the phrase (AP, AdvP, or NP), not the single-word category, and begin the clause S there.

In order to determine which kind of node (AP, AdvP, or NP) should be above the S, just ask yourself the adjective, adverb, and noun questions and review the list of subordinating conjunctions.

Parsing and Treeing Sentences with Subordinate Clauses

1. <u>We</u> <u>will give</u> candy (to [<u>whoever</u> <u>comes</u> (to the door)]). The complement (noun) clause does not need any further labeling because it is the object of the preposition *to*.

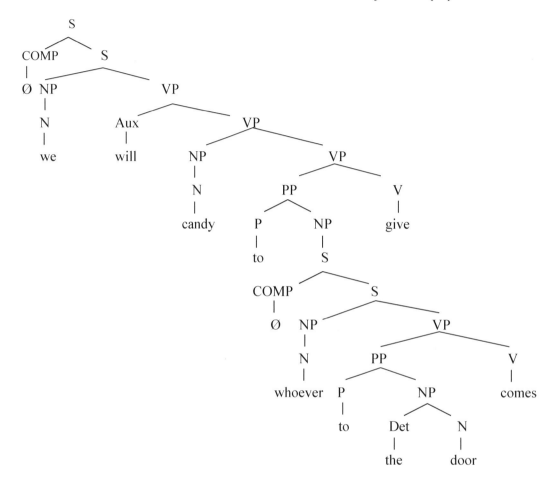

Even though you might be tempted to use 'whomever' instead of 'whoever' because it follows the preposition *to*, you can see that it is the subject of the subordinate clause and must therefore take the subjective, or nominative, case. Because *whoever* is the subject NP of the subordinate clause, it is already in initial position and does not need to move into COMP.

2. <u>Tristan can play</u> [when <u>he is finished</u> (with his homework)]. Remember that A stands for adverb clause and R stands for relative clause (adjective).

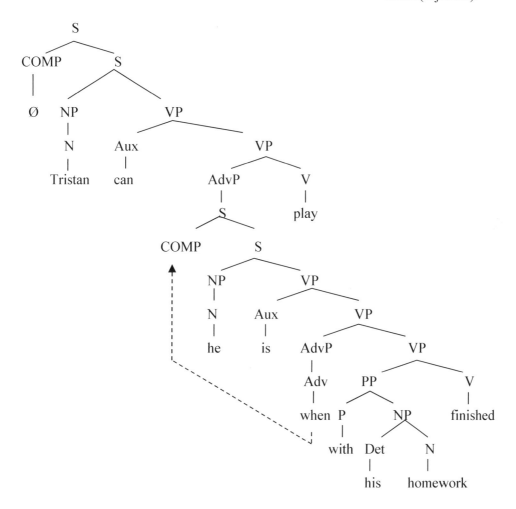

If you treated *finished* like a predicate adjective instead of a main verb, that would be fine. Either way, it is the past participle form of the verb 'to finish'. As a predicate adjective, it would be a static participle; as a main verb, it would be an eventive participle. In English we do not think of the fine semantic (meaning) difference between static participles and eventive participles because the form is the same for both. However in some languages, for example the Slavic languages, the verb forms would be different from one another, and both speakers and listeners would be conscious of the difference in meaning. They would think of Tristan either as in the state of being finished (static) or experiencing the final moment of finishing (eventive).

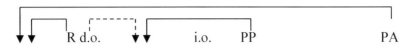

3. The <u>necklace</u> [that <u>John</u> <u>gave</u> his girlfriend (for her birthday)] <u>was</u> expensive. The d.o. marks the word *that*, and the R marks the entire clause. You may, if you wish, run a dotted line from the indirect object to the verb, but it is not necessary because the indirect object will automatically be tied to the same verb as the direct object.

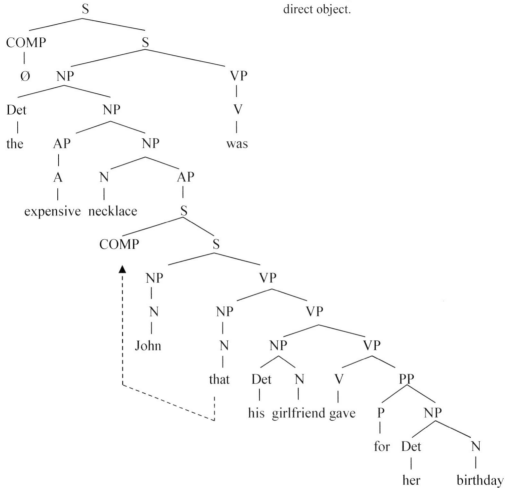

Remember that a pronoun takes the place of a noun. In this sentence, the relative pronoun *that* takes the place of *the necklace* in meaning. Therefore the underlying structure of the subordinate clause is 'John gave his girlfriend that for her birthday', meaning 'John gave his girlfriend the necklace for her birthday'. *That* then moves out of direct object position to the beginning of the subordinate clause to satisfy the surface structure rule that a subordinate clause must begin with a subordinating conjunction.

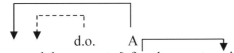

4. <u>They</u> <u>opened</u> the presents [after the <u>guests</u> <u>arrived</u>]. When the subordinating conjunction is adverbial, it will **always** point to the predicate of the subordinate clause.

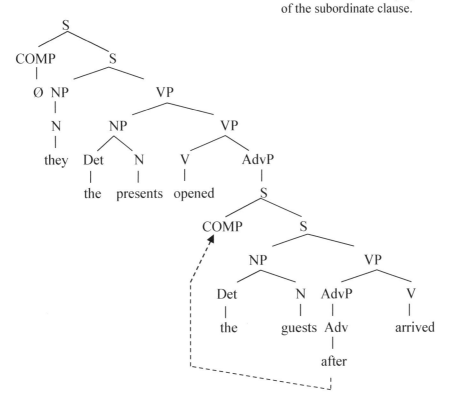

Will anything ever move into the COMP position at the top of the tree? It will. In Wh-questions, such as 'who are you?', the Wh- interrogative moves into COMP, and the subject and predicate are inverted.

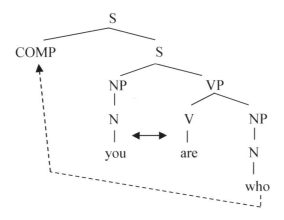

5. <u>They</u> <u>like</u> [whomever <u>they</u> <u>met</u> (at George's party) (on Saturday)].

If you included *on Saturday* within the other PP and had it modifying *party*, you still have standard usage. It would give the sentence a slightly different meaning, however. The sentence here stresses that Saturday was when they met the person or people whom they like. Including *on Saturday* within the other PP, on the other hand, would imply that George gives a lot of parties and that it was the one on Saturday at which they met the person or people whom they like.

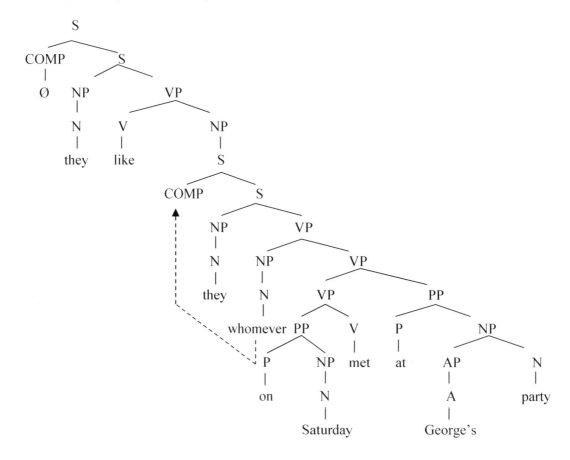

One way to make sure that you have the proper number of nodes coming off of the VP is to check the number of arrows pointing to the verb in the parsed sentence. Each word pointing to a verb should be in a node coming off of a VP. Remember that even though they are not connected with arrows, indirect objects and predicate nouns should also be in nodes coming from the VP.

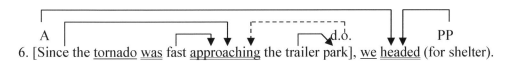

6. [Since the <u>tornado</u> <u>was</u> fast <u>approaching</u> the trailer park], <u>we</u> <u>headed</u> (for shelter).

Fast can be either an adjective, as in *the fast car*, or an adverb as it is here.

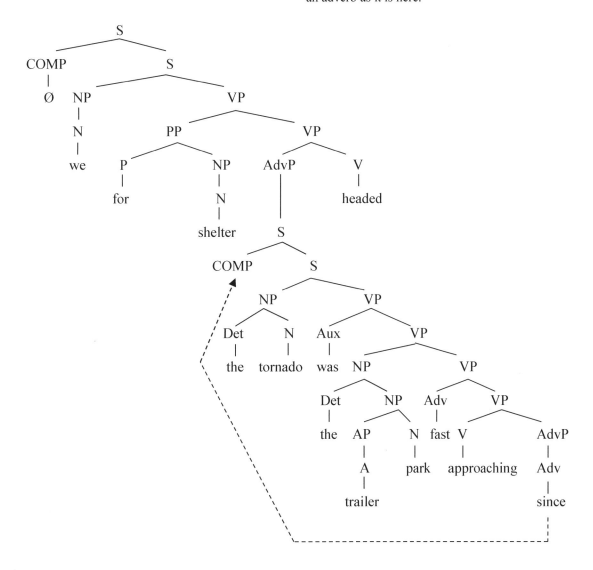

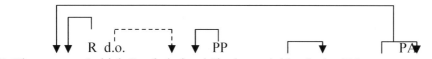

7. The <u>sweater</u> [which <u>Sandy</u> <u>knitted</u> (for her neighbor's dog)] <u>is</u> very warm.

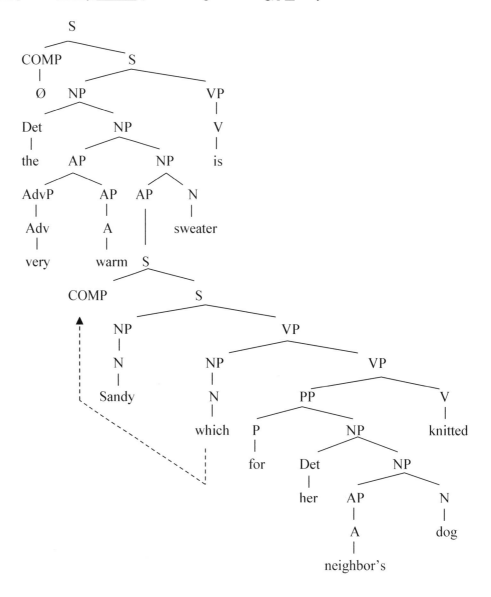

83

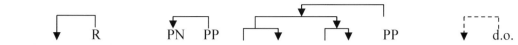

8. <u>Jack Colby</u>, [who <u>became</u> one (of the most famous hog ropers (in history,))] <u>loves</u> horses.

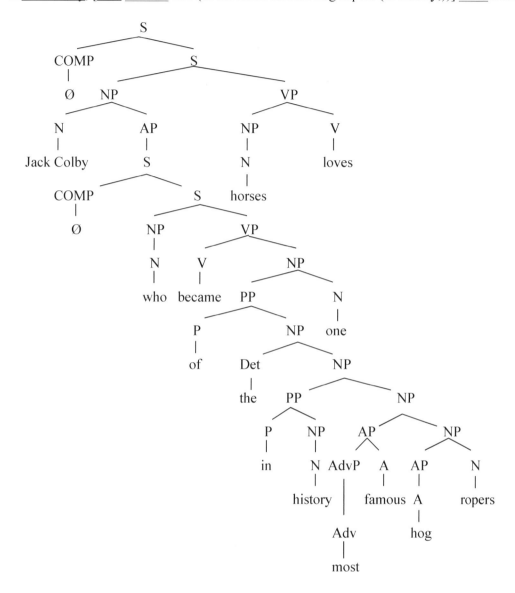

84

Practice with Clauses

Review

Relative clauses: act as adjectives
modify nouns
tell which one, what kind of
are labeled R in parsing
are APs and therefore come off of NPs in a tree

Adverb clauses: act as adverbs
usually modify verbs
tell when, where, why, how, to what extent, under what conditions
are labeled A in parsing
are AdvPs and therefore come off of VPs in a tree

Complement clauses: act as nouns
tell who[m] or what
are labeled C in parsing
are NPs and therefore come off of Ss, VPs, or PPs

Relative clauses

1. The book which you gave me did not interest me.
2. Kelly wants a new swing set for the children whom she babysits.
3. Ian plays in a band that performs for weddings.
4. Are you the person I saw at the bank?

Adverb clauses

1. Until I met you, I always canoed the river by myself.
2. Talina talks negatively about other people because her parents did the same thing.
3. When they look like anvils, cumulous clouds usually bring thunder and lightning.
4. We will be late for the concert unless this traffic jam disperses.

Complement clauses

1. I wonder what he is doing now.
2. Do you know when I started this project?
3. Benji goes to whoever feeds him.
4. Eileen cannot remember how she got to the mall.

Key to Practice with Clauses

Relative clauses

1. The <u>book</u> [which <u>you</u> <u>gave</u> me] <u>did</u> not <u>interest</u> me. If you check the number of arrows pointing to verbs against the number of nodes coming from the VP, be sure to count indirect objects even though they do not need arrows.

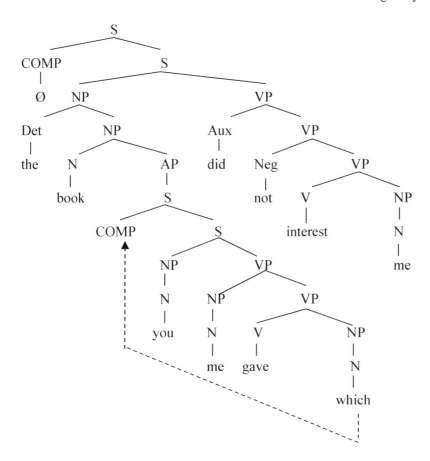

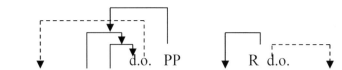

2. <u>Kelly</u> <u>wants</u> a new swing set (for the children [whom <u>she</u> <u>babysits</u>]). Pay careful attention to parenthesis and bracket placement.

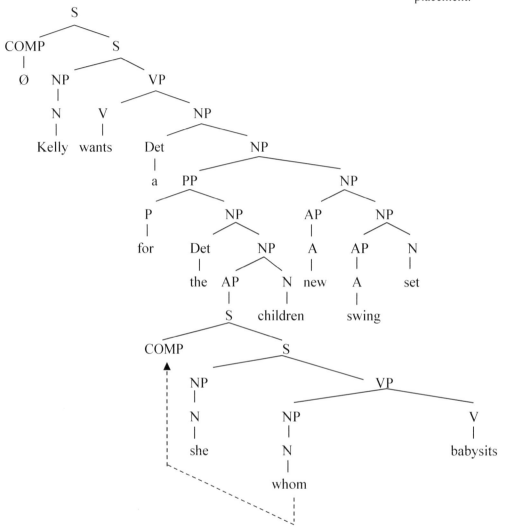

87

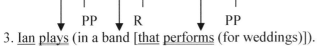

3. <u>Ian</u> <u>plays</u> (in a band [<u>that</u> <u>performs</u> (for weddings)]).

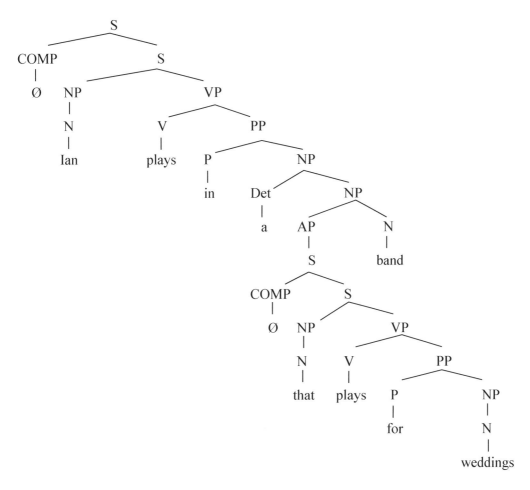

There is no dotted line here because the subordinating conjunction *that* is the subject NP of the clause and already occupies initial position.

PN↓   R   ↓   PP

4. <u>Are</u> <u>you</u> the person [<u>I</u> <u>saw</u> (at the bank)]? In informal writing and speaking the subordinating conjunction is sometimes left out of relative clauses. But remember always to include it in formal usage.

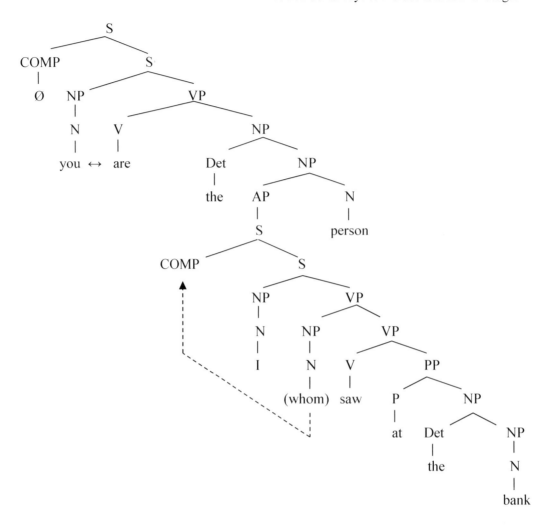

<u>Adverb clauses</u>

1. [Until <u>I</u> <u>met</u> you], <u>I</u> always <u>canoed</u> the river (by myself). There are four arrows pointing to *canoed*, so there should be four nodes coming from the VP besides the V.
By myself does not tell what kind of river. It tells how I canoed.

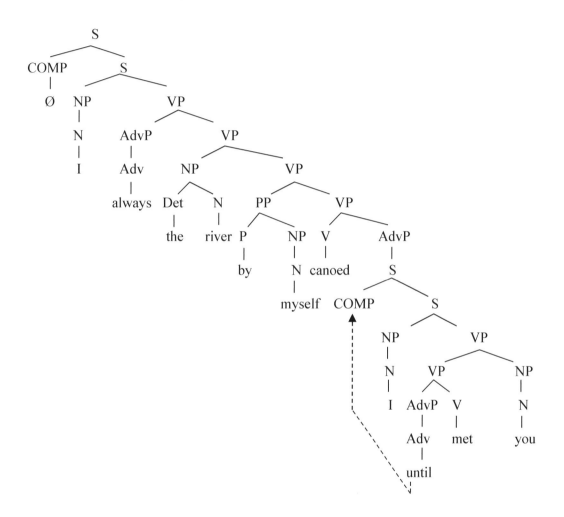

2. <u>Talina</u> <u>talks</u> negatively (about other people) [because her <u>parents</u> <u>did</u> the same thing].

When an adverb subordinate clause appears at the beginning of a sentence, it is followed by a comma; when it appears at the end of a sentence, there is no comma in front of it.

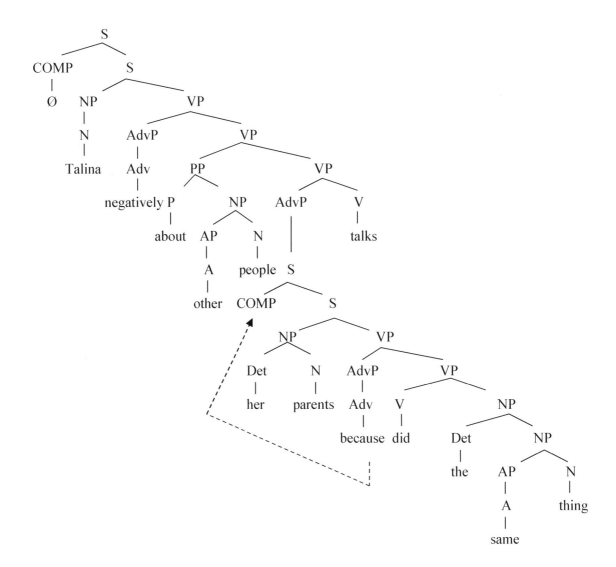

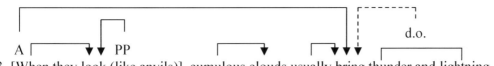

3. [When <u>they</u> <u>look</u> (like anvils)], cumulous <u>clouds</u> usually <u>bring</u> thunder and lightning.

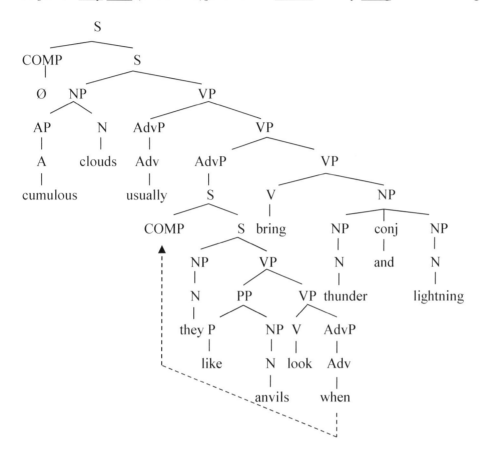

92

4. <u>We</u> <u>will be</u> late (for the concert) [unless this traffic <u>jam</u> <u>disperses</u>].

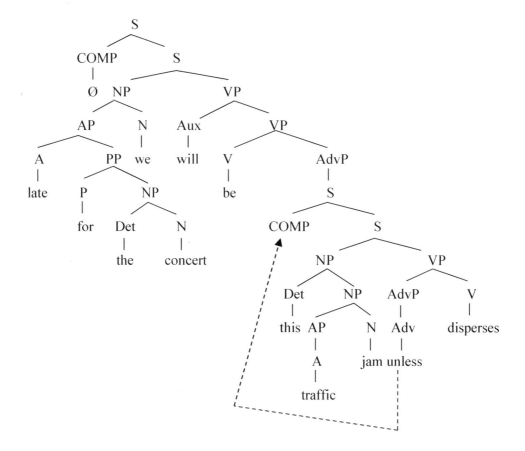

93

Complement clauses

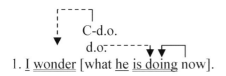

1. I wonder [what he is doing now].

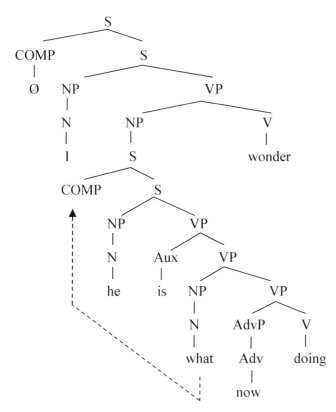

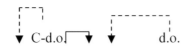

C-d.o.   d.o.

2. <u>Do</u> <u>you</u> <u>know</u> [when <u>I</u> <u>started</u> this project]?   Even though the subordinate clause is a complement (noun), the subordinating conjunction is adverbial. The clause tells what, and the conjunction tells when.

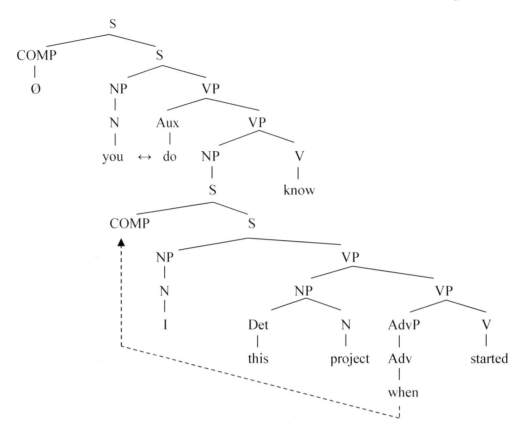

95

PP C   d.o.
3. <u>Benji</u> <u>goes</u> (to [<u>whoever</u> <u>feeds</u> him]).

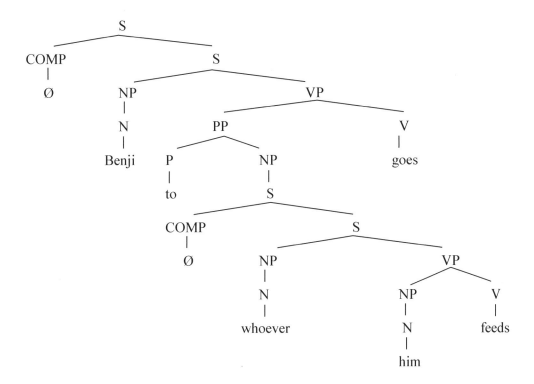

A tree is an abstraction of the possible underlying grammatical structures of English. Not all possible nodes are filled with words in every sentence, which accounts for the null symbols.

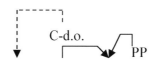

4. <u>Eileen</u> <u>cannot remember</u> [how <u>she</u> <u>got</u> (to the mall)].

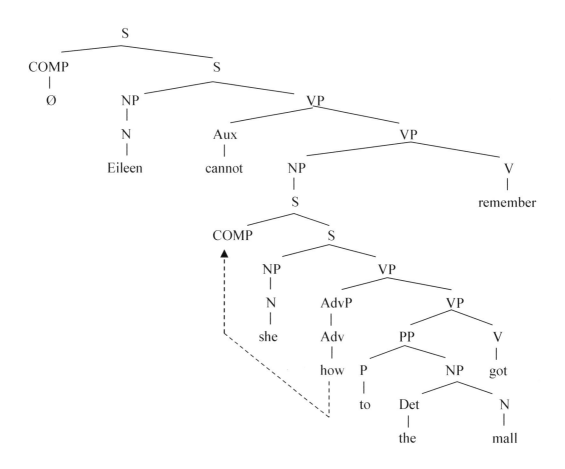

97

Verbals

Review the forms and functions of the three verbals on the traditional grammar outline—forms, so that you can recognize what they look like, and functions, so that you know how they relate to other structures in a sentence.

Remember: A verbal **functions** as a noun, adverb, or adjective; but intrinsically it is still a verb, and as such it may do anything other verbs do—have subjects (except for participles), objects, and modifiers. A **verbal phrase** is the verbal plus its subject, object, and modifiers.

Participles = adjectives

1. crawling through the brush	The boy X ripped his pants.
2. slashed by heavy winds	X the trees were destroyed.
3. taking responsibility for her actions	X she confessed to the student body.
4. given the circumstances	X, we granted her amnesty.

Gerunds = nouns

1. taking responsibility for her actions	X was a welcome sign of maturity.
2. crawling through the brush	He hates X.
3. his giving her the ring	The biggest surprise was X.
4. making the dean's list	Since X, Jan has become more studious.
5. locking him in his room	You could give X a try.

Infinitives =
- nouns

1. to become president of the club	X was his goal.
2. to bake a pie	He learned X.
3. to die peacefully	Her greatest wish is X.

- adverbs

1. to attract young women	He dyes his hair X.

- adjectives

1. to make friends	This is the best way X.

Parsing and Treeing Verbals

Being phrases, verbals are parsed with parentheses just like PPs are parsed; however, they may also have direct or indirect objects, predicate nouns, or adverbs which need to be accounted for.

In underlying structure verbals are like subordinate clauses in that they are treed as Ss. The only difference is that clauses must always have a word or phrase in the NP subject position whereas verbals may or may not. This is because the definition of a clause is a group of words having a subject and a predicate. Predicates must contain finite verbs. Verbals, on the other hand, are nonfinite verbs and do not need subjects. When gerunds and infinitives do have NP subjects, they are not in the nominative case. Participles never have subjects.

The NP subject of an **infinitive** is in the **objective case**.

inf.

Infinitive with no subject: <u>He</u> <u>wants</u> (to go).

inf.

Infinitive with subject: <u>He</u> <u>wants</u> (me to go). *Me* is the subject NP of *to go*.

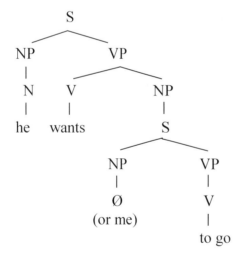

The NP subject of a **gerund** is in the **possessive case**.

Gerund with no subject: I $\underset{\text{ger.}}{\underline{\text{admire}}}$ (skating).

Gerund with subject: I $\underset{\text{ger.}}{\underline{\text{admire}}}$ (his skating). *His* is the subject NP of *skating*.

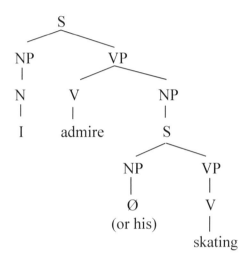

Distinguishing between Participles and Gerunds

Notice that 'crawling through the brush' can be either a participle or a gerund. By definition, if it acts as an adjective in the sentence, it is a participle; if it acts as a noun, it is a gerund. Even though verbals are verbs, they are not predicates because they do not have tense. Therefore, they are not underlined twice in parsing. The following two sentences demonstrate:

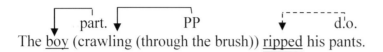

The <u>boy</u> (crawling (through the brush)) <u>ripped</u> his pants.

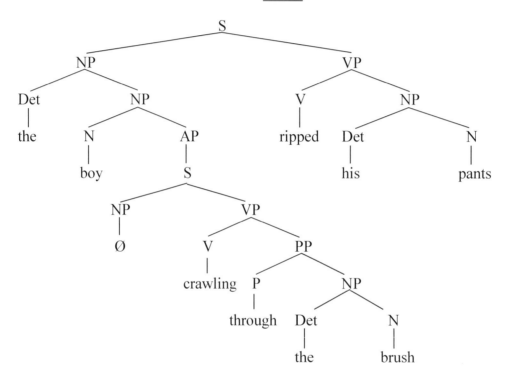

Surface structure determines whether the participle is restrictive or nonrestrictive because of its position in the sentence, but underlying structure does not. A restrictive modifier is necessary to specify the referent of the noun that it modifies. A nonrestrictive modifier simply adds description to the modified noun. Postpositioning (following the noun) makes the participle restrictive: it distinguishes this boy who is crawling through the brush from some other boy who did not rip his pants. If the participle were prepositioned (preceding the noun), it would be nonrestrictive and would be followed by a comma.

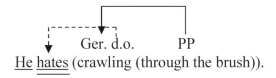

<u>He</u> <u>hates</u> (crawling (through the brush)).

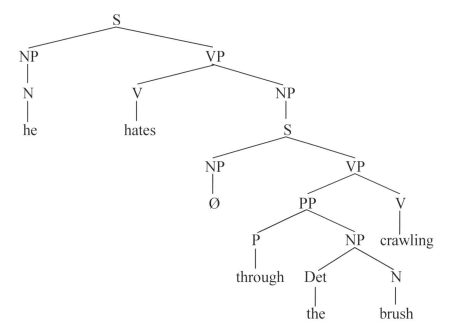

Practice Parsing and Treeing Verbals

1. Stepping gingerly, the thief crept across the floor.

2. Johnson decided to take his son to the football game.

3. She drinks to forget.

4. He needs a reason to study.

5. Skiing is his favorite sport.

6. Wrapping the woolen shawl about her shoulders, the old woman opened the door of

her cabin and faced the blizzard.

7. Alta wants to go to the mall, but Sevi prefers watching TV.

8. The blowing snow blinded Hassan, causing him to veer off the road.

9. We will never be able to thank Cheng enough for his being there.

Key to Practice Parsing and Treeing Verbals

1. (Stepping gingerly), the <u>thief</u> <u>crept</u> (across the floor). Participles that begin a sentence will often be followed by a comma, and they will always modify the next noun, which will probably be the subject.

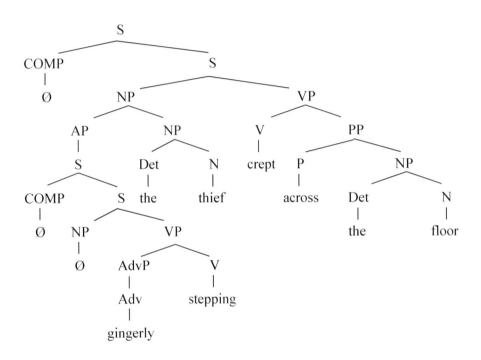

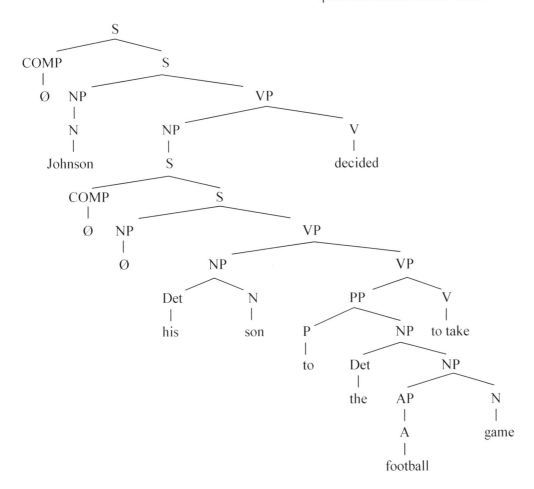

2. <u>Johnson</u> <u>decided</u> (to take his son (to the football game)). The entire verbal phrase is *to take his son to the football game*, and it is the direct object of *decided*, answering the question Johnson decided what?

In many of the trees drawn here, the NP direct object (*his son* in this tree) is on the left side of the V in the VP (*to take*). Do not let this confuse you into thinking that the NP direct object is the subject of the verb. The only reason for this placement is simply to fit the tree onto the page. The NP subject of the clause or verbal will always come directly off of an S, never a VP.

inf.

3. <u>She</u> <u>drinks</u> (to forget). The infinitive is acting as an adverb that tells why she drinks.

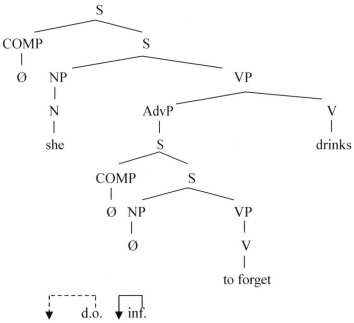

d.o. inf.

4. <u>He</u> <u>needs</u> a reason (to study). The infinitive is adjectival because it tells what kind of reason.

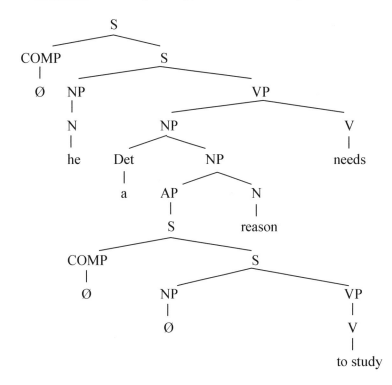

ger.   ↱ PN
5. (Skiing) is his favorite sport.

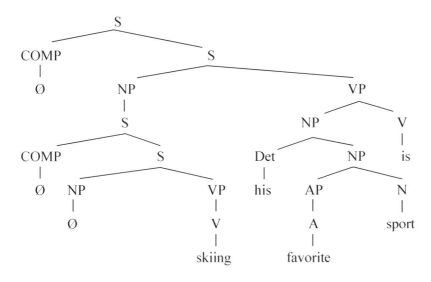

Remember that predicate nouns, or predicate nominatives, are treed just like direct objects. The difference between predicate nouns and direct objects only matters in surface structure; the trees do not care about case. As you can guess from their names, predicate nominatives are in the nominative case, and direct objects are in the objective case. In English all of the case endings on common nouns have disappeared over the centuries. The only remaining remnants of case difference can be seen in the pronouns (page 3). What distinguishes a predicate nominative from a direct object in surface structure is simply whether or not it follows a copular verb. Trees do not care whether a verb is a copula or not. But in order to choose the proper pronoun in surface structure, you must know whether that pronoun is a predicate nominative or a direct object: 'It was they who wrecked their car' rather than 'It was them who wrecked their car' uses the proper case form because *was* is a copular verb, making *they* a predicate nominative.

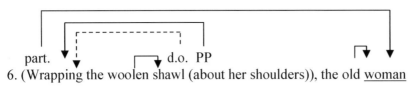

6. (Wrapping the woolen shawl (about her shoulders)), the old <u>woman</u>

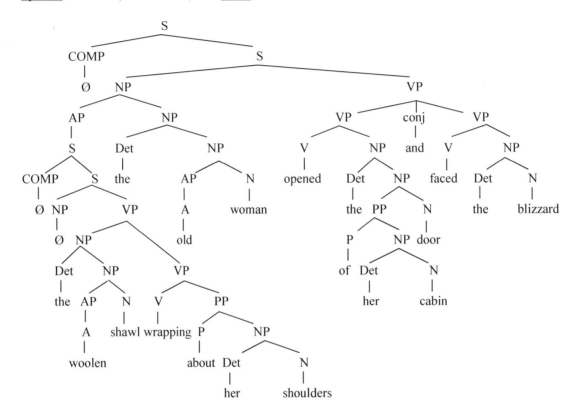

<u>opened</u> the door (of her cabin) and <u>faced</u> the blizzard.

7. <u>Alta</u> <u>wants</u> (to go (to the mall)), but <u>Sevi</u> <u>prefers</u> (watching TV). Notice that a verbal acts like its function as a noun, adverb, or adjective in relation to words outside the verbal phrase but acts like a verb within its verbal phrase. Therefore it can be a direct object to the main verb at the same time that it can take its own direct object within its verbal phrase.

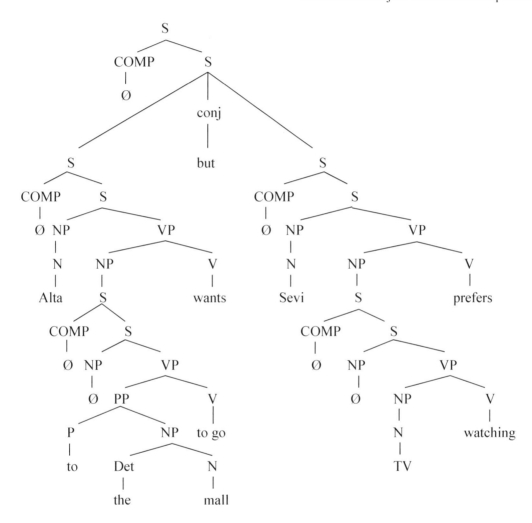

108

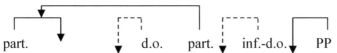

part.   d.o.   part.   inf.-d.o.   PP

8. The (blowing) <u>snow</u> <u>blinded</u> Hassan, (causing (him to veer (off the road))).

The questions which one and what kind of do not always identify participles logically. Instead, think of who or what is doing the action that the participle describes. That is the word that the participle modifies. Therefore, what is it that is blowing? the snow; what is it that is causing him to veer off the road? the blowing snow.

In this sentence the infinitive happens to have a subject. Review pages 99-100.

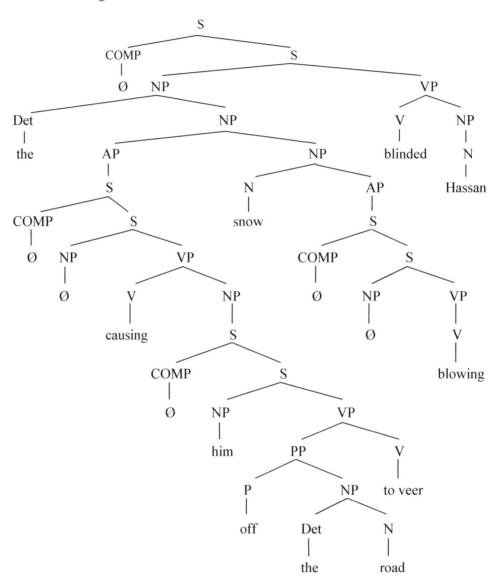

9. <u>We</u> <u>will</u> never <u>be</u> able (to thank Cheng enough (for (his being there))). *Not* is considered a negative, but *never* is an adverb, meaning 'not ever' and telling when. *Able* describes we (it is not a verb—'enable' is a verb). The infinitive phrase tells how able. The subject of a gerund phrase is always in the possessive case.

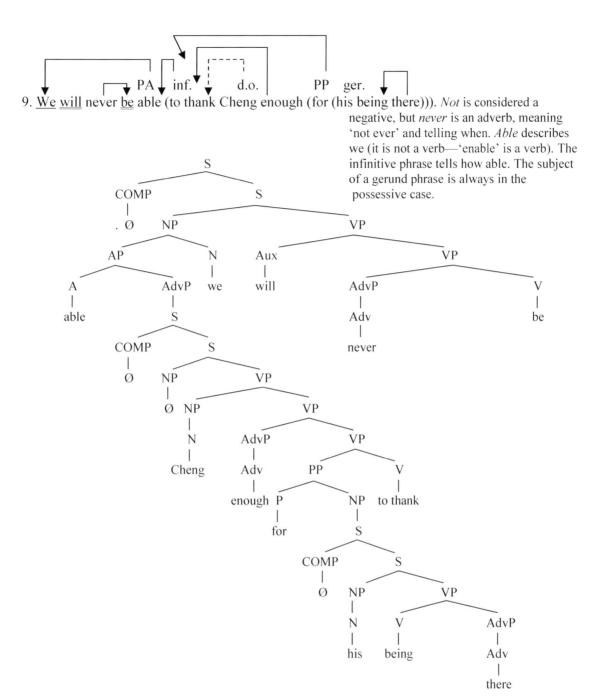

110

Practice Parsing and Treeing Sentences with Verbals and Clauses

1. I wonder when the group that we paid to see will start singing.

2. Which book are we supposed to bring to class today?

3. Bonnie picked up the little kitten, which she heard crying in the tall grass.

4. Trying to make a sale, the John Deere implement distributor told us that he would give us a discounted price.

5. Learning to knit was Gloria's New Year's resolution because she wanted to make her boyfriend a sweater.

6. King crab legs are Erika's favorite meal, so she always orders them when she goes to Jaker's.

7. The Olympic committee, which had taken Bright Path's medal from him, finally returned it to him, restoring honor to his name.

8. Whoever put this worm into my cole slaw wants to be a comedian.

Key to Parsing and Treeing Sentences with Verbals and Clauses

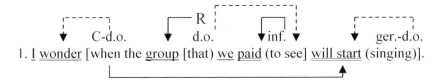

1. I wonder [when the group [that) we paid (to see] will start (singing)].

The C clause answers the question, I wonder what. The R clause tells which group. Its underlying structure is 'we paid to see that (the group)'. *To see* tells why we paid. *Singing* answers the question, group will start what. Even though the C clause is a noun, it begins with an adverbial conjunction, which must modify the predicate within its clause, *will start*.

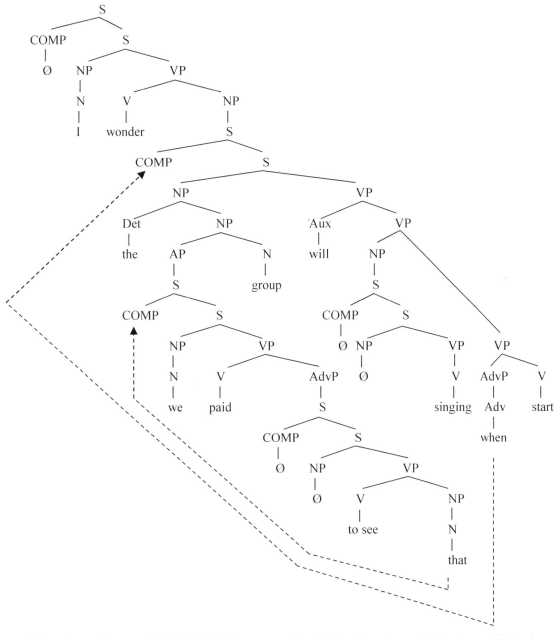

How do you know which COMP *when* moves into? Check and see which clause it introduces, and move it into the COMP coming off of that S.

2. Which book <u>are</u> <u>we</u> <u>supposed</u> (to bring (to class) today)? The underlying structure would be 'we are supposed to bring which book to class today'. When *supposed* is used with an infinitive, it is somewhat idiomatic, and the logic of determining *to bring* as the direct object is less obvious. You could think, is supposed to do what. Or you could try the list of adverbial questions (suppose when, suppose where, suppose why, etc.) and arrive at the what question by process of elimination. *Today* is an adverbial noun, which parses like an adverb and trees like a noun.

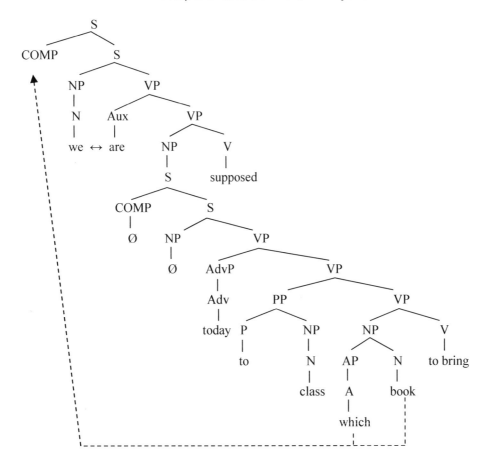

113

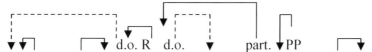

3. <u>Bonnie</u> <u>picked</u> up the little kitten, [which <u>she</u> <u>heard</u> (crying (in the tall grass))].

Up is an adverb modifying *pick* rather than a preposition. Technically, it is called a particle. Remember that a preposition has to have an object, and *kitten* is not the object of *up*. One way to distinguish a particle from a preposition is to see if the word can be moved to the end of the clause. Prepositions cannot leave the beginnings of their phrases, but adverbs are more free to move. You could say 'Bonnie picked the little kitten up', but you could not say 'crying the tall grass in'.

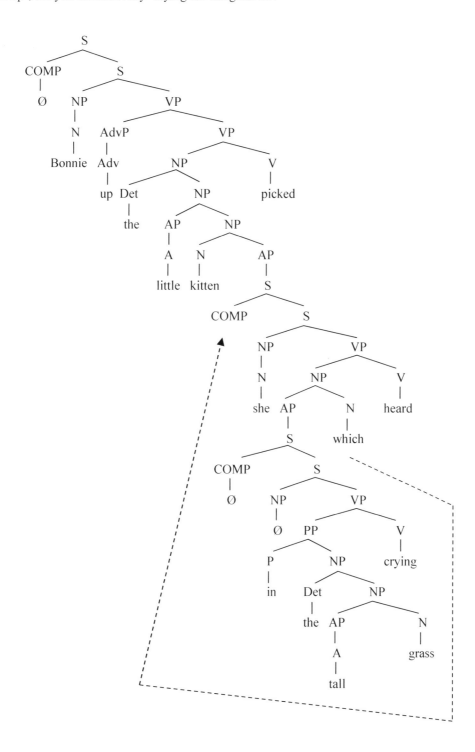

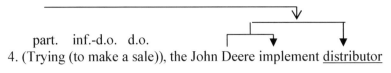

part.   inf.-d.o.   d.o.

4. (Trying (to make a sale)), the John Deere implement <u>distributor</u>

Discounted is a past participle.

i.o. C-d.o.   i.o.   part.   ▼d.o.

<u>told</u> us [that <u>he</u> <u>would give</u> us a (discounted) price.

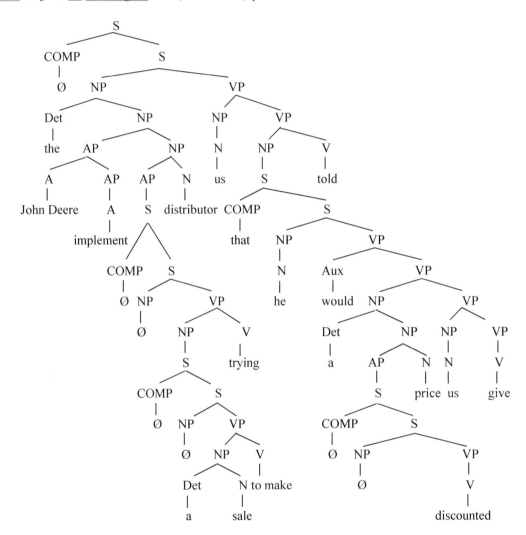

That in this sentence is a throwback to older forms of English. It is neither a subject nor an object and does not move into COMP from other positions. It just goes there directly. It would never appear in a sentence in which another conjunction needed to move into COMP.

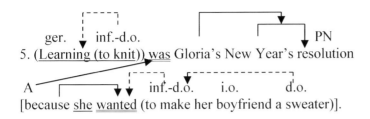

5. (Learning (to knit)) was Gloria's New Year's resolution [because she wanted (to make her boyfriend a sweater)].

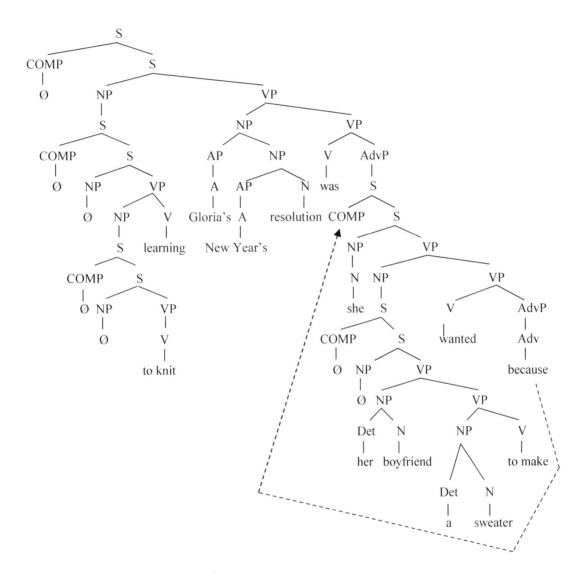

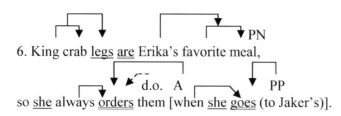

6. King crab <u>legs</u> <u>are</u> Erika's favorite meal,
so <u>she</u> always <u>orders</u> them [when <u>she</u> <u>goes</u> (to Jaker's)].

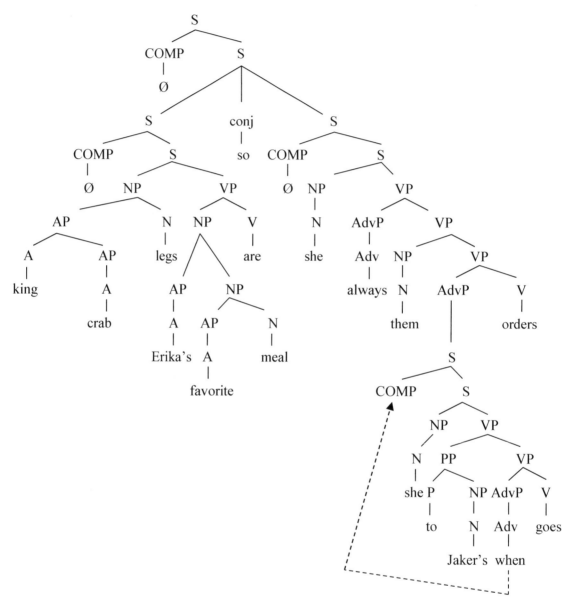

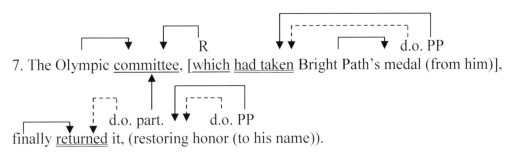

7. The Olympic <u>committee</u>, [which <u>had taken</u> Bright Path's medal (from him)],

finally <u>returned</u> it, (restoring honor (to his name)).

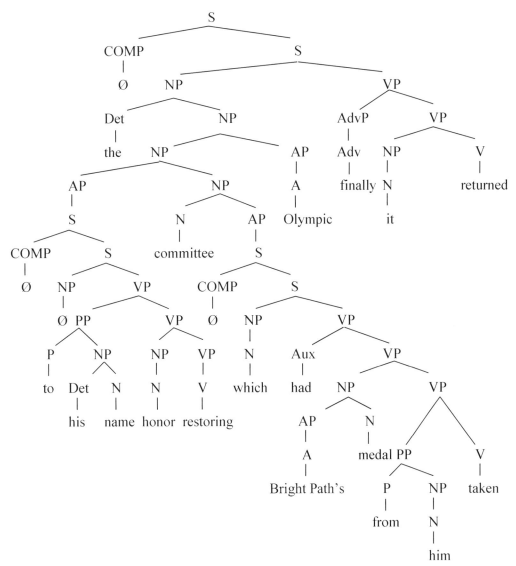

The NPs on the subject side of the sentence are zigzagged for no other reason than to fit the tree on the page. Remember that the order of nodes does not matter laterally (left and right). Tree structure shows the hierarchical pattern of a sentence, and therefore it only matters which nodes are above and below one another.

C   d.o.   PP   inf.-d.o.   PN

8. [<u>Whoever</u> <u>put</u> this worm (into my cole slaw)] <u>wants</u> (to be a comedian).

The entire C is the subject of the sentence.

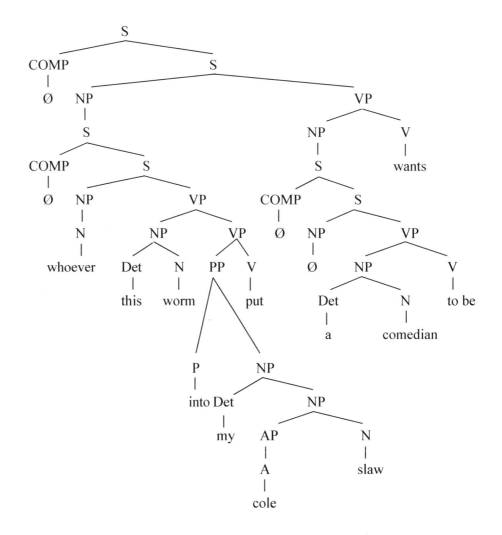

119

SENTENCE TYPES

There are four sentence types: simple, compound, complex, and compound-complex.

A **simple sentence** has one independent clause and no dependent clauses.
The gray squirrel ran up the tree.

A **compound sentence** has two or more independent clauses and no dependent clauses.
The gray squirrel ran up the tree, and the black Labrador chased it.

A **complex sentence** has one independent clause and one or more dependent clauses.
The gray squirrel ran up the tree because the black Labrador was chasing it.

A **compound-complex sentence** has two or more independent clauses and one or more dependent clauses.
The gray squirrel ran up the tree because the black Labrador was chasing it, but the dog was too slow to catch the squirrel.

Compound Sentence Elements and Compound Sentences

Coordinating conjunctions are used to join compound structures. These structures may be sentence elements or sentences themselves.

Compound sentence elements (these all happen to be simple sentences)

                                                          PP
Compound subject: Mary and John went (to a movie).
                                                          d.o.
Compound predicate: The team rallied and won the game.

(Notice that 'game' is the direct object of 'won' but not 'rallied'. The team did not rally the game.)

                                                      d.o.   d.o.
Compound direct object: Wisconsin has a state bird and a state flower.
                                                         p.a.   p.a.
Compound predicate adjective: She always looks really sharp or really sloppy.
                                                 PP   PP
Compound prepositional phrase: Go (through that door) and (to the left).

Compound sentences

        d.o. PP   PP   d.o.   PP
Jack made a lot (of noise (about the bad call)), but he did not do anything (about it).
                                    d.o.   d.o.
The home builder could raise his prices, or he could sell the business.
                 p.a.   PP   PP
Jody would be late (for class), so he just stayed (in bed).

Practice Quiz on Sentence Types

Underline the subject once and the predicate twice in each of the **clauses** below. Put parentheses around subordinating conjunctions. Then identify the sentences as simple (S), compound (C), Complex (CX), or compound-complex (CCX). If the selection is not a sentence, mark it as a fragment (F).
Insert commas and semicolons where necessary.

____ 1. Until he realized the difficulty of the situation the firefighter was relatively relaxed with his assignment.

____ 2. Josh just did not know what he should do.

____ 3. Josh just did not know what to do.

____ 4. Wanting to change her life and become born again the woman in the front row quickly rose with the others to approach the minister on the stage.

____ 5. Tami called a taxi because she could not remember where she had parked her car.

____ 6. At the beginning of the play the Shakespearean language confused our guests but by the beginning of the second act they could understand everything perfectly.

____ 7. The red Mazda and the Chevy with a 456 engine were both in the shop at the same time.

____ 8. Chenile thought that her dog would have to be put to sleep but her friend told her about a vet who could perform hip surgery that was ninety percent effective.

____ 9. When we went out on the boat the water was rougher than I have ever seen it.

____ 10. I wished that I could have been there for the party until I saw how you looked the next day.

____ 11. How much time do you spend watching TV every day?

____ 12. If it were not for you I would still be utterly confused about what is going on in this class.

____ 13. Because there was very little time left and nothing that he could do about it.

____ 14. Jamie and Clare are going to the library do you want to study in the lounge?

____ 15. Tokay is served in Eastern Europe as a dessert wine.

____ 16. If you ever get a chance to travel to Greece be sure to tour the islands.

____ 17. Jerad is an excellent athlete but not a team player.

____ 18. Dillon won four blue ribbons with his animals at the county fair and then decided to sell them in order to add to his college tuition fund.

____ 19. Not if she is going to treat me like a criminal just because I came home late a couple of times.

____ 20. Then he decided to leave.

____ 21. That was then this is now.

____ 22. Although it was not the first time that his mother had given him that warning.

____ 23. Can you give me an update a little later?

____ 24. Do you know what time it is?

____ 25. Both the regular professor and the person asked to substitute for a day required the students to show the processes on their math problems.

Key to Quiz on Sentence Types

Underline the subject once and the predicate twice in each of the **clauses** below. Then identify the sentences as simple (S), compound (C), Complex (CX), or compound-complex (CCX). If the selection is not a sentence, mark it as a fragment (F).
Insert commas and semi colons where necessary.

__CX__ 1. (Until) he realized the difficulty of the situation, the firefighter was relatively relaxed with his assignment.   1 independent, 1 dependent clause

__CX__ 2. Josh just did not know (what) he should do. 1 independent, 1 dependent clause

__S__ 3. Josh just did not know what to do.   1 independent clause

__S__ 4. Wanting to change her life and become born again, the woman in the front row quickly rose with the others to approach the minister on the stage.   1 independent clause

__CX__ 5. Tami called a taxi (because) she could not remember (where) she had parked her car.   1 independent, 2 dependent clauses

__C__ 6. At the beginning of the play, the Shakespearean language confused our guests; but by the beginning of the second act, they could understand everything perfectly.
        2 independent clauses

__S__ 7. The red Mazda and the Chevy with a 456 engine were both in the shop at the same time.   1 independent clause with a compound subject

__CCX__ 8. Chenile thought (that) her dog would have to be put to sleep, but her friend told her about a vet (who) could perform hip surgery (that) was ninety percent effective.
        2 independent, 3 dependent clauses

__CX__ 9. (When) we went out on the boat, the water was rougher (than) I have ever seen it.   1 independent, 2 dependent clauses

__CX__ 10. I wished (that) I could have been there for the party (until) I saw (how) you looked the next day.   1 independent, 3 dependent clauses

__S__ 11. How much time do you spend watching TV every day?   1 independent clause

__CX__ 12. (If) it were not for you, I would still be utterly confused about (what) is going on in this class.   1 independent clause, 2 dependent clauses

__F__ 13. (Because) there was very little time left and nothing (that) he could do about it.
        1 dependent clause within another dependent clause

123

_C_ 14. Jamie and Clare are going to the library; do you want to study in the lounge?
  2 independent clauses

_S_ 15. Tokay is served in Eastern Europe as a dessert wine.
  1 independent clause

_CX_ 16.(If) you ever get a chance to travel to Greece, (you) be sure to tour the islands.
  1 independent, 1 dependent clause

_S_ 17. Jerad is an excellent athlete but not a team player. 1 independent clause with a
  compound predicate noun

_S_ 18. Dillon won four blue ribbons with his animals at the county fair and then decided
to sell them in order to add to his college tuition fund.   1 independent clause with a
  compound predicate

_F_ 19. Not (if) she is going to treat me like a criminal just (because) I came home late a
couple of times.   1 dependent clause within another dependent clause

_S_ 20. Then he decided to leave.   1 independent clause

_C_ 21. That was then; this is now.   2 independent clauses

_F_ 22. (Although) it was not the first time (that) his mother had given him that warning.
  1 dependent clause within another dependent clause

_S_ 23. Can you give me an update a little later?   1 independent clause

_CX_ 24. Do you know (what) time it is?   1 independent, 1 dependent clause

_S_ 25. Both the regular professor and the person asked to substitute for a day required
the students to show the processes on their math problems. 1 independent clause with a
  compound subject

STANDARD USAGE

What you have learned thus far is the grammar of English—its structure. Most people misuse the term 'grammar.' When they say that a person has good or bad grammar, what they are actually referring to is usage. 'Good grammar' is standard usage; 'bad grammar' is nonstandard usage. Just as people have preconceived notions about you because of your regional accent, they will also judge you by your use of standard or nonstandard English. The important thing to remember is that language use is not good or bad. It is appropriate or inappropriate. As is mentioned in the introduction, your language is like your clothing. You do not dress formally all of the time, and you do not need to use 'who' and 'whom' properly all of the time. You dress for the occasion; your language should also fit the occasion. At best, not knowing standard English will limit the types of social situations in which you can feel comfortable. At worst, it could cost you a job or desirable personal relationship.

Spelling

Most spelling errors are caused by carelessness. Spell check will change words that do not exist into words that do exist, but that does not mean they will be correct. Of course, hand-written documents, messages, and notes are totally your responsibility. Thus, you need to proofread your writing carefully. Reading your document out loud is a good way to proofread. Reading it backwards will help you notice words that are spelled incorrectly, but it will not help you notice words that are out of context. One of the most common spelling errors occurs with words that sound alike but are often confused, such as *affect* and *effect*; another is with words that double or do not double the last consonant before adding an –ing, –ed, or –er ending.

Words Often Confused

accept, except
Accept is a verb; *except* is not.
I *accept* your invitation.   Everyone came to the meeting *except* him.

advise, advice
Advise is a verb; *advice* is a noun.
The professor *advises* students, but they rarely need *advice*.

affect, effect
Affect is always a verb; effect is almost always* a noun.
The crops were *affected* by lack of rain.   Sugar has a negative *effect* on your teeth.
*When *effect* is a verb, it means 'to bring about'.
This legislation will *effect* a boost in the economy by raising the minimum wage.

all ready, already
If you leave out *all* and the sentence still makes sense, *all ready* is the correct form to use.
      I'm *already* gone.   Dinner is *all ready*.

choose, chose
Choose is present tense; *chose* is past tense.
Today I *choose*; yesterday I *chose*.

clothes, cloths
If you pronounce these words properly, you should not have any trouble spelling them correctly. The *e* in *clothes* makes the *o* sound like /o/; *cloth* rhymes with moth.
He likes to wear his brother's *clothes*.   The moth ate a hole in the *cloth*.

coarse, course
Coarse means 'rough'; a *course* is what you take in school or a path to follow.
The sandpaper is *coarse*.   They laid out the *course* for the race.

compliment, complement
Compliment means praise. Remember '*I* like compl*i*ments'.
Complement means something that completes or brings to perfection. All but the last two letters of *complete* are in the word *complement*.
Complimenting people will help you make friends.
That necklace *complements* your outfit.

conscious, conscience
Conscious means 'aware'; your *conscience* is Jiminy Cricket on your shoulder telling you what is right and wrong.
She was not *conscious* of his presence. Her *conscience* is bothering her because she lied.

dessert, desert
You want two helpings of *dessert*, so give it two *s*'s; all other meanings are spelled with one *s*.   We had pie for *dessert*. The *desert* is cold at night. Don't *desert* me!

fourth, forth
Fourth has the word four in it; otherwise use *forth*.
That was his *fourth* home run.   Go *forth* and prosper.   They went back and *forth*.

its, it's
Its is a possessive pronoun; *it's* is a contraction of 'it is'.
The dog is chasing *its* tail.   Buckle up—*it's* the law.

lead, led
Lead is pronounced /lɛd/ only when it refers to the metal. As the present tense verb it is pronounced /lid/. *Led* is the past tense of *lead* and rhymes with the metal pronunciation.
Get the *lead* out!   Today the band is *leading* the parade.   Yesterday we *led* the singing.

loose, lose
Loose is pronounced with an /s/; *lose* is pronounced with a /z/.
He is *loose* as a goose.   Try not to *lose* this book.

passed, past
Passed is a verb; use *past* when it is not a verb.
They *passed* the truck going ninety and went right *past* a highway patrol car in the median.

piece, peace
Remember 'a *pie*ce of *pie*' and visualize whirled *pea*s (world *pea*ce).

personal, personnel
Pronounce these correctly, and you will not make a mistake spelling them. *Personal* has the stress on the first syllable, and *personnel* has it on the last.
I sent a *personal* note to my physical therapist to thank him for helping me after the accident.   Please report to the *personnel* office to fill out some forms.

principal, principle
Principal means 'main'. Remember the *principal* (main official in school) is your *pal*. A *principle* is a 'rule.' Both words end in *-le*.
The *principal* difficulty is finding adequate personnel. He is a man of *principles*.

quiet, quite
Misspelling these words is usually a matter of carelessness. Pronounce them correctly, and you should not have any problems. *Quiet* has two syllables.
For Jennifer to be *quiet* for more than ten minutes is *quite* a feat.

than, then
Than compares two or more things; *then* refers to time.
Duct tape costs less *than* chemical wart removers. That was *then*; this is now.

their, they're, there
Their is a possessive; *they're* is a contraction of *they are*; *there* refers to a place. Compare *their* with *its* and *they're* with *it's*.
Their daughter will graduate next year. *They're* very proud of her. Will you be *there*?

to, too, two
To is a preposition or part of an infinitive; *too* means 'very' or 'also'; *two* is a number.
He is *too* vain *to* realize that having *two* girlfriends is not fair *to* either of them.

weather, whether
Weather refers to atmospheric conditions; *whether* means 'if'.
Whether he goes to the ball game depends on the *weather*.

whose, who's
Whose is a possessive; *who's* is a contraction of *who is*.
Whose party will you go to this weekend?   She is the person *who's* going to tutor me.

127

your, you're

Your is a possessive; *you're* is a contraction of *you are*.
You're the master of *your* own fate.

Doubling the Final Consonant

Double the final consonant when adding an ending beginning with a vowel, such as –ing, -ed, or –er, if the word
1. ends in a single consonant
2. which is preceded by a single vowel
and
3. is stressed (accented) on the last syllable.

Examples:

begin   1. It ends in a single consonant—*n*
             2. which is preceded by a single vowel—*i*
             3. and has the stress on the last syllable.
Therefore, double the *n* in *beginning* and *beginner*.

stop   1. It ends in a single consonant—*p*
             2. which is preceded by a single vowel—*o*
             3. and has the stress on the last syllable (the only syllable).
Therefore, double the *p* in *stopping*, *stopped*, and *stopper*.

benefit   1. It ends in a single consonant—*t*
             2. which is preceded by a single vowel—*i*
             3. but the stress is not on the last syllable.
Therefore, do not double the *t* in *benefiting* or *benefited*.

roar   1. It ends in a single consonant—*r*
             2. but it is not preceded by a single vowel.
Therefore, do not double the *r* in *roaring* or *roared*.

talk   1. It does not end in a single consonant.
Therefore, do not double the *k* in *talking*, *talked*, or *talker*.

Note: *Qu-* is treated as /kw/. In other words, the *u* is not considered a vowel when it follows *q*. Therefore, we double the *t* in *quitting* and *quitter*. Likewise, *w* at the end of a word is not considered a consonant (*bow* /bo/), and *x* at the end of a word is considered /ks/.

100 Most Often Misspelled Words

A variety of websites publish lists of commonly misspelled words, often with mnemonic devices for remembering how to spell them correctly. To identify those which are difficult for you, have a friend give you an oral test. Then print the list and highlight those which you need to learn.

Contractions, Possessives, and Plurals

The apostrophe in a **contraction** indicates that a letter or letters have been left out: isn't, you've, he's, I'd, don't, let's, etc.

Possessive nouns (not pronouns) are formed by adding *'s* or *s'*. Historically, this apostrophe also indicated that a letter had been left out. In Middle English, the genitive case (possessive) ended in *–es*. Because these possessive forms were often confused with plural forms, it became customary to replace the *e* with an apostrophe in possessive forms. When you need to form a possessive, ask yourself this question: "Who does it belong to?" (Since you're talking to yourself, you don't need to use 'whom'.) If the answer to your question does not end in *–s*, add *'s*. If the answer to your question does end in *–s*, then only add *'*.

Examples:

Jacks apartment	Jack's
James apartment	James'
the Smiths cat	Smiths'
the womans song	woman's
the womens song	women's

Plural forms end in *–es* when the last sound in the singular form is /s/ or /z/. All other regular nouns end in *–s*. Irregular plurals are throwbacks from Old and Middle English. Mass nouns, such as 'wheat', do not form plurals.

Examples:

glass	glasses
quiz	quizzes
bat	bats
box (/baks/)	boxes
pear	pears
child	children
sheep	sheep (historically a mass noun because it was a flock)

Punctuation and Capitalization

Although there may be some minor discrepancies, editing formats such as MLA, APA, ACA, and the Chicago Style Sheet agree on punctuation rules. Punctuation marks are like road signs in that they alert the reader to the structure of the sentence up ahead. If you do not want readers to accidentally misinterpret your writing, you must put in the proper punctuation marks.

Commas ,

1. Use commas to separate items in a series.
>He ordered pepperoni, sausage, and mushrooms on his pizza.

2. Use a comma before a coordinating conjunction (page 20) that joins two independent clauses.
>The rookie golfer won his first tournament, and the crowd went wild.

3. Do not use a comma to separate other compound structures.
>The truck driver filled out his log book and then went into the cafe for lunch.

4. Use a comma after an adverb clause that comes at the beginning of a sentence, but do not use a comma before an adverb clause that comes at the end of a sentence.
>Because it had snowed overnight, she decided to go skiing instead of studying.
>She decided to go skiing instead of studying because it had snowed overnight.

5. Use a comma to set off expressions that interrupt the sentence.

Appositives: The chief firefighter, Pete Holcomb, received a plaque for his service.

Words in direct address: You, my friend, are asking for trouble.

Short direct quotations: They said, "Don't get near that fire," as the flames leapt higher.

Parenthetical expressions (unless parentheses are used): He avoided all spicy food, such as pizza and chili.

Nonrestrictive clauses and participial phrases: That guy in the red shirt, which looks way too big for him, runs the mile.   The irate child, screaming and kicking, was completely ignored by his mother.

6. Do not use a comma with restrictive clauses or participial phrases.
>That guy who runs the mile is wearing a shirt that looks way too big for him.
>The mother completely ignored her screaming and kicking child.

7. Use a comma to avoid confusion or misreading of the sentence.
>Screaming and kicking, the child was ignored by his mother.

8. Use commas to set off every item after the first in dates and addresses.
>She lives at 245 Pine Street, Tulsa, OK.
>The twins were born on September 25, 2002, in Lethbridge, Alberta.

9. Use a comma after an introductory phrase six words or longer.
>While opening the envelope from her grandmother, Janine got a paper cut.

10. Do not use a comma to separate main sentence elements, for example subjects, predicates, and direct objects.
>Robin worked with her horse every day and came away from the rodeo with a first place in barrel racing.

Semicolons ;

1. Use a semicolon between two independent clauses that are not joined by coordinating conjunctions.

     The clerk had an opinion about her customer's color choice but chose not to mention anything; it was better left unsaid.

2. Use a semicolon between independent clauses joined by conjunctive adverbs, such as *accordingly, also, besides, consequently, furthermore, hence, however, indeed, instead, moreover, nevertheless, otherwise, similarly, still, therefore, thus, for example, for instance, that is,* and *in fact.* Because conjunctive adverbs can also be used as interrupters in single clauses, be sure of the sentence structure.

     They wanted to take the train to Seattle; however, the fare was too outrageous.

     They decided, therefore, to stay home.

3. Use a semicolon between independent clauses if one or both of them contain commas.

     The newly-engaged couple, who were shopping for wedding rings, visited four jewelry stores but could not find a style that pleased them both; at last they settled on plain gold bands.

4. Use a semicolon between the items in a series if any of the items contain commas.

     Jeanine's reasons not to take a trip during spring break were that she was nearly broke; her friends, who all had jobs, could not take off work for a week; and she needed the time to catch up on school work.

Colons :

Use a colon <u>after a complete statement</u> when a list or long quotation follows.

     We bought a lot of new equipment for our backpacking trip: a lightweight tent, sleeping pads, rain ponchos, and a cook kit.

     Yogi Berra had this to say about putting: "Ninety-three percent of short putts never go in the hole."

Periods .

Use a period to end a sentence and after an abbreviation.

     I would like you to meet Mr. and Mrs. Jones.

Question Marks ?

Use a question mark after a direct question but not after an indirect one.

     "When do you expect to be home?" she asked.

     She asked when he expected to be home.

Italics **and** <u>**Underlining**</u>

Use italics when keyboarding, and use underlining when writing in long hand to identify novels, CDs, movies, anthologies, and other long works which are published under their own covers.

     "Youth," by Joseph Conrad, appears in the collection *Tales of Unrest.*

Double Quotation Marks " "

1. Put double quotation marks around the exact words of a speaker but not around an indirect statement.

> Alexander Pope said, "To err is human; to forgive is divine."
> Aristotle said that all men are mortal.

2. Put double quotation marks around the titles of stories, songs, poems, essays, or other short works which are contained within larger publications.

> The little girl played "Gaviotte" for her piano recital.

3. Commas and periods go inside quotation marks; semicolons and colons go outside quotation marks. Question marks go inside if the question is part of the quotation and outside if it is not.

> For his homework he had to read "Metamorphosis."
> "This car," the salesman continued, "has all the bells and whistles."
> The title of her essay was "John Deere Green"; in it she explored the effects of equipment costs on the economics of farming.
> The narrator reveals several personality traits in "My Last Duchess": jealousy, the need to control, vanity, brutality, and artful conversation.
> "Where Have All the Flowers Gone?" was a mild protest song of the sixties.
> What historical error is evident in Keats' "On First Looking into Chapman's Homer"?

Single Quotation Marks ' '

Use single quotation marks around a quote within a quote.

> The professor asked her students, "How many of you read 'Stopping by Woods on a Snowy Evening' in high school"?

Capital Letters

1. Capitalize the first letter in a sentence.

> We rode our bikes to town.

2. Capitalize proper nouns.

> John, Mariah, and Betsy flew to Cracow and stayed at the Hotel Biala.

3. Capitalize the first and last word of a title plus all other words except prepositions, articles, and conjunctions.

> The Incredible Lightness of Being

4. Capitalize the first word in a direct quotation.

> "That is an amazing trick," said the magician, "simply amazing."

Parentheses ( )

Parenthetical remarks may be asides or clarifying phrases.

> The old man (he was eighty if he was a day) would not give up his independence.
> The uvula (hangy-down thing) is often confused with the tonsils.

Parentheses are also used for in-text references in academic writing.

> Johnson (2009) shows that caffeic acid, not caffeine, is present in apples.

Adjectives and Adverbs

If you look back at the phrase structure rules (page 40), you will see which categories are modified (described) by adjectives and which are modified by adverbs. Adjectives **modify** nouns and other adjectives. Adverbs modify verbs, adjectives, and other adverbs. Adverbs that modify adjectives, such as *too* and *very*, are sometimes called **intensifiers**.

A large number of adverbs are formed by adding the *–ly* morpheme to an adjective, such as *heavy, heavily; quiet, quietly;* and *serious, seriously*. Special attention, however, should be paid to irregular forms, such as *good* (adj.) and *well* (adv.). To use adjectives and adverbs properly, you must know which forms are which and what word they are modifying. Going by what sounds good is not a smart idea because adjectives and adverbs are used informally rather often in everyday speech. Therefore, what sounds good, or familiar, is likely to be nonstandard.
Examples:

> That guy can jump *really high*. (not *real high*)
> You did *really well* on that test. (not *real good*)
> He *surely* is gaining a lot of weight. (not *sure*)
> She put the brakes on too *quickly* and spilled our drinks. (not *quick*)

Agreement

Between Subject and Predicate

Subjects and predicates must agree in number. That means that if the subject is singular, the singular form of the verb must be used; if the subject is plural, the plural form of the verb must be used. Second language learners find this concept confusing because plural nouns are often formed with *–s*, and third person singular verbs often end with *–s*. Native speakers usually have less trouble with the forms, but identifying the subject of a clause sometimes gives them problems. Indefinite pronouns pose particular problems of their own. Refer to the list on the next page.
Examples:

> Near the fireplace <u>were</u> two overstuffed <u>chairs</u>.
> There <u>were</u> several <u>students</u> waiting to get into the room.
> <u>Each</u> of the teams <u>has</u> a warm-up routine.
> <u>All</u> of the pie <u>is</u> gone.
> <u>All</u> of the dogs <u>are</u> in their kennels.

When there is a compound subject conjoined by *or* and one of the elements is singular while the other is plural, make the predicate agree with the element which is closer to it.

> Either the <u>Crupper twins or Benji</u> <u>is going</u> to ride on the float.
> Either <u>Benji or the Crupper twins</u> <u>are going</u> to ride on the float.

133

Between Pronoun and Antecedent

A pronoun is a word that takes the place of a noun. The noun it replaces is its antecedent. Pronouns and their antecedents must agree in number and, in the case of singular forms, gender. Because women's issues have become so prominent in American society, the older practice of using masculine pronouns to refer to all humans has given way to the practice of recognizing pronominal gender differences in their singular forms. However, whether you adopt the newer practice or adhere to the older one, you will be making a political statement. In your own writing if you are not sure which political statement you want your reader to hear, the best practice is to use plural forms, where gender differences are not linguistically evident. *His or her* and *his/her* are other options. Examples:

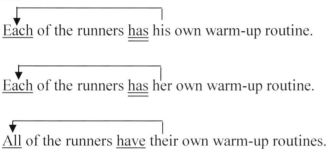

Each of the runners has his own warm-up routine.

Each of the runners has her own warm-up routine.

All of the runners have their own warm-up routines.

Here is a list of indefinite pronouns to help you remember which are singular and which are plural. Those which can be either singular or plural are determined by the context (usually the object of the preposition in the preceding phrase) of the sentence.

Singular

each	either	everybody	somebody
anybody	nobody	everyone	someone
one	neither	anyone	no one

Plural

several	few	both	many

Singular or Plural

some	any	none	all	most

Examples:
Everybody must have his or her own eating utensils for the outing.

Has anyone finished writing his/her autobiographical sketch yet?

Some of the people are discussing their opinions on global warming.

Some of the lecture is repetitious.

134

It seems odd, but grammatically "everybody" and "everyone" are singular rather than plural. Think of them as "each person" and "each one." Making the subject and predicate agree is easy because it sounds right, but making the pronoun and antecedent agree is more difficult. The following sentence is correct: Everybody has his or her own book. Most people would say (and write) 'Everybody has their own book'. They would not use "have," the plural form of the verb, but they do use "their," the plural form of the pronoun. Before political correctness became an issue in language choice, we would have said 'Everybody has his own book'. Using he/she and his/her is cumbersome, but since most people are not aware of their readers' political sensitivities and do not want to offend, they generally make the effort. A handy alternative is to use a plural subject if at all possible: All of the students have their own books.

When prepositional phrases are involved, making subjects agree with their predicates and pronouns can be tricky. I have underlined the subjects, double underlined the predicates, and shaded the pronouns in the following sentence and put (parentheses) around the prepositional phrase. The predicate and pronouns must agree with the subject in number.

Each (of the students) is giving his or her report this week.

Although you may be tempted to make the predicate and pronouns agree with "student" rather than "Each," this would be incorrect: *Each of the students are giving their report this week. (An asterisk indicates a nonstandard sentence.)

Remember that all of the indefinite pronouns that are always singular or always plural must always take singular or plural predicates regardless of the prepositional phrases which follow them. However, the indefinite pronouns listed as either singular or plural depend upon the prepositional phrases which follow them. If the noun that is the object of the preposition is singular, then use a singular predicate; if the noun that is the object of the preposition is plural, then use a plural predicate.

Some (of the pie) is gone.   Some (of the students) are gone.

Is any (of our money) left in the kitty?   Are any (of my coins) still on the dresser?

All (of the yard) has been raked.   All (of the leaves) have been raked.

The last bit of trickiness occurs when "either/or" and "neither/nor" are used with a compound subject. In this case, make the predicate agree with the nearest member of the compound.

Either he or they are going to be blamed.
Either they or I am going to be blamed.

Neither Jack nor his brothers are coming for dinner.
Neither the Jackson twins nor Tim is coming for dinner.

Case

Case tells you who did what to whom. In English the word order of the sentence is responsible for making these relationships clear to the reader. The subject usually comes first, then the verb, and then the direct object. Languages that are **inflectional** have much less restrictive word orders because their grammars are more flexible; they make it possible for their writers to use techniques that beautify the language and imply more subtle meanings. Inflectional languages indicate the **case** of a noun usually with a morphemic ending on the word. Therefore, a noun is free to appear anywhere in the sentence order because its intrinsic form indicates whether it is the subject, direct object, predicate noun, indirect object, or object of preposition. In English, on the other hand, we must interpret these relationships from context and word order.

Since English has lost most of its inflections, we do not need to worry about the morphological endings of nouns except with possessives, where genitive case is indicated by *'s*. We still have some case distinctions with pronouns, however, and this is where you need to know how a word functions in the sentence. Look back at the pronoun grid on page 3. English pronouns have subject (nominative), object (a variety of cases in other languages), and possessive forms. These correspond to semantic and grammatical roles in the sentence. The nominative form pronouns are used for subjects and predicate nominatives in clauses. The object forms are used for direct objects (accusative case), indirect objects (dative case), objects of prepositions (locative, ablative, and instrumental are common cases in this category), and NPs of infinitives. Possessive forms are used for NPs of gerunds. The pronoun use that sounds 'right' to you will depend on your family as well as the social class and regional area in which you developed your language habits. Pronoun case probably provides the most nonstandard usage in everyday English. In order to be confident with the standard usage of pronoun case, you must rely on your knowledge of the grammatical structure of sentences.

Practice with Case #1

When you do these exercises, tell what function the pronoun has in the clause: subject, predicate nominative, direct object, indirect object, object of preposition, NP of infinitive, or NP of gerund.

1. It was to Lillian and (I, me) that this letter was sent.
2. Tell them that (we, us) rooters won't let them down.
3. That may have been (he, him) on the stairs.
4. Do you know what time (he, him) and (she, her) plan to arrive?
5. I've known Polly and (she, her) for as long as I can remember.
6. We can always be sure of a good performance from Roger and (they, them).
7. Because of (he, him) they won the final game.
8. Neither you nor (I, me) can predict the future.
9. Let Bruce and (he, him) do the job in their own way.
10. I will tell you my decision, but keep it just between you and (I, me).
11. This coat doesn't fit either you or (she, her).
12. If I were (he, him), I would go at once.

13. Where could we find another shortstop like Bob or (he, him)?

14. For (we, us) younger drivers the cost of automobile insurance is especially high.

15. Was it (they, them) you told me about yesterday?

16. For the two singing parts, Miss Jensen chose Joan and (she, her).

17. Who will help Louise and (she, her) with the work?

18. The speakers at the meeting will be you and (he, him).

19. My brother and (I, me) have always competed against each other.

20. The work on the project was done by both Isabel and (I, me).

21. Women built like you and (she, her) should never wear long-waisted dresses.

22. During the study period Bert and (I, me) had a chance to compare notes.

23. When the coach calls upon (we, us) second-stringers, we must be ready.

24. They told both (he, him) and (I, me) that we had been elected.

25. Are you sure it was (she, her) who came yesterday?

26. How could they ever mistake (we, us) for one another?

27. I'm sure that the winner will be (he, him).

28. Mr. Howells wants either Jeff or (I, me) at the meeting.

29. I told Marcia and (she, her) as much of the story as I knew.

30. Perhaps neither the Millers nor (they, them) will be living on this block next year.

31. Are you going to let this come between you and (I, me)?

32. Give David and (he, him) whatever they need to get started.

33. Can (we, us) women help them in the kitchen?

1.	me, o.p.	2. we, sub.	3. he, p.n.	4. he - she, sub.	5. her, d.o.
6.	them, o.p.	7. him, o.p.	8. I, sub.	9. him, NP of inf. (*to* do)	
10.	me, o.p.	11. her, d.o.	12. he, p.n.	13. him, o.p.	14. us, o.p.
15.	they, p.n.	16. her, d.o.	17. her, d.o.	18. he, p.n.	19. I, sub.
20.	me, o.p.	21. her, o.p.	22. I, sub.	23. us, o.p.	24. him - me, i.o.
25.	she, p.n.	26. us, d.o.	27. he, p.n.	28. me, d.o.	29. her, i.o.
30.	they, sub.	31. me, o.p.	32. him, i.o.	33. we, sub.	

Practice with Case #2

1. Have you met Perry and (he, him)?
2. The coach wants you and (I, me).
3. Miss Smith asked Marie and (she, her) to help her with the yard work.
4. Bill and (I, me) did the homework together.
5. Was it you or (he, him) who solved the first problem?
6. I am expecting you and (she, her).
7. (He, Him) and (I, me) took the late bus.
8. I don't know (who, whom) the pitcher was.
9. It was she (who, whom) I told you about.
10. The manager hired both Ellen and (I, me).
11. He will support (whoever, whomever) supports him.
12. Jerry and (they, them) are coming later.
13. I know (who, whom) you were talking to.

14. Please take Ann and (I, me) with you.
15. The fight was between Sanford and (he, him).
16. Mrs. Thompson invited (we, us) men into her office.
17. We'll take (whoever, whomever) comes first.
18. Tell Joan and (I, me) the whole story.
19. (We, Us) women were sitting on the front porch.
20. He spoke to Sam and (I, me).

1.   him, d.o.   2. me, d.o.   3. her, NP of inf.   4. I, sub.   5. he, p.n.
6.   her, d.o.   7. He - I, sub. 8. who, p.n.   9. whom, o.p. 10. me, d.o.
11. whoever, sub. 12. they, sub. 13. whom, o.p. 14. me, d.o.   15. him, o.p.
16. us, d.o.   17. whoever, sub. 18. me, i.o. 19. We, sub.   20. me, o.p.

Elliptical Sentences

An ellipsis in normal text consists of three or four dots, which usually indicate that part of a quotation has been left out. **Elliptical sentences** are those in which part of a clause has been left out. When it comes to pronouns, you need to mentally fill in the missing part of the sentence in order to make the right case choice.

Example: He has not gained as much weight as I (have gained). *I* is in the nominative case because it is the subject of the elliptical clause *as I have gained*.

In some instances, particularly with comparatives which can act either as subordinating conjunctions or as prepositions, the sentence can be interpreted in two ways. If the comparative is intended as a subordinating conjunction, then the following pronoun is most likely the subject of the elliptical clause. If the comparative is intended as a preposition, then the following pronoun will be the object of that preposition.

Examples: No one worked harder than I (worked). 'than' is a subordinating conjunction
             No one worked harder than me. 'than' is a preposition

In the examples above, there is no significant change in meaning. In some sentences, however, the choice in pronoun either changes the meaning or makes the sentence nonstandard.

Examples: I told you more than he (told you).
             I told you more than (I told) him.
             Did you study as long as we (studied)?
         .   *Did you study as long as us?
             An asterisked * sentence is nonstandard and should be corrected.
             'Did you study as long as you studied us' is a possible interpretation, but
             logic tells us that this is not the intended meaning of the sentence.

Practice with Case #3

1. No one worked harder than (I, me).

2. Did you do better than (she, her)?

3. She did more for Mary than (I, me).

4. The boys on our team are faster than (they, them).

5. We ate more pizza than (they, them).

6. My brothers boasted that they were stronger than (we, us).

7. She thought she could swim farther than (I, me).

8. I need you as much as (he, him).

Key to Practice with Case #3

1. either, no change in meaning

2. either, no change in meaning

3. I, sub. (than I did for Mary); me, o.p. (than she did for me)

4. either, no change in meaning

5. they, sub. ('me' would be grammatically correct but semantically undesirable)

6. either, no change in meaning

7. either, but with a slight change in meaning

   Choosing 'I' would mean that she thought she could swim a farther distance than I could swim at any time. Choosing 'me' would mean that she thought she could swim farther than the point at which I am treading water right now.

8. I, sub. (as he needs you); him, d.o. (as I need him)

Note: When making case choices with pronouns, be aware that some speakers consider the use of comparatives as subordinating conjunctions to be more formal than as prepositions.

Misplaced and Dangling Modifiers

We have two types of modifiers in English, adjectives and adverbs. Adverbs are relatively flexible in English word order. That is, they can appear at the beginning or end of a sentence and before or after a verb. Adjectives, on the other hand, are more strictly regulated in their position. In standard usage, an adjective should be next to the noun that it modifies. **Misplaced modifiers** are adjective clauses or phrases (single word adjectives are rarely misplaced) that have been placed next to nouns that they are not supposed to modify, therefore violating the logic of the sentence.

Examples:
>*Harry and Vicki like to play cribbage, who are my neighbors.
>Harry and Vicki, who are my neighbors, like to play cribbage.
>*Running down the field, the mother cheered for her son.
>The mother cheered for her son, who was running down the field.
>Running down the field, the boy could hear his mother cheering for him.

Dangling modifiers are usually participial phrases which do not logically modify any word in the sentence. The concept of a noun may be in the mind of the reader, but grammatically the participle is dangling because it has no noun to modify.

Examples:
>*Swimming as hard as we could, our lungs ached and seemed about to burst.
>Swimming as hard as we could, we felt as though our aching lungs would burst.
>Because we were swimming as hard as we could, our lungs ached and seemed about to burst.
>*Our passports needed to be ready, driving across the border.
> Driving across the border, we needed to have our passports ready.
>Our passports needed to be ready as we drove across the border.

Parallel Construction

As you saw in the phrase structure rules, when you joined two structures they had to be the same. You could not join an NP and an AP with a Conj, for example. What this means in the traditional terminology of standard English is that whenever you join two or more elements to form a compound, those elements must have the same grammatical structure.

Examples:
>*It is important to have fun as well as making good grades in college.
>Having fun in college is as important as making good grades.
>*His favorite recreational activities are football, skiing, and riding his bike.
>His favorite recreational activities are playing football, skiing, and riding his bike.
>*She rarely spoke about her loneliness, depression, and how tired she always felt.
>She rarely spoke about how lonely, depressed, and tired she always felt.
>*Before she could go to work, she had to dress her children, make breakfast for them, and then she had to pack their lunches.
>Before she could go to work, she had to dress her children, make their breakfast, and pack their lunches.

Practice Quiz #1 on Spelling

Add –ing to the following words according to the rules for doubling the last consonant.

1. defer	6. par
2. begin	7. detour
3. compel	8. order
4. bludgeon	9. scar
5. program	10. return

Key to Practice Quiz #1 on Spelling

1. deferring	6. parring
2. beginning	7 detouring
3. compelling	8. ordering
4. bludgeoning	9. scarring
5. programing*	10. returning

*You have no doubt seen 'programing' spelled with two m's. This derives from the British infinitive form, which is spelled 'programme'. If you follow the rules for doubling the last consonant, however, you will <u>not</u> double the 'm' because the accent is on the first syllable of the word.

Practice Quiz #2 on Spelling

Circle the correct word in parentheses.

1. Everyone appreciates a (complement, compliment) once in a while.

2. My house payment includes only forty dollars of the (principal, principle).

3. No one likes a (deserter, desserter).

4. Our state is having a difficult time (choosing, chosing) its electors.

5. That man is having a strange (affect, effect) on me.

6. Are you (all ready, already) to go?

7. Kalina loves school (accept, except) when she has to take a test.

8. (Its, It's) important to distinguish between love and pity.

9. He (lead, led) in popular votes, but she acquired the electors.

10. Torina spends more time socializing (than, then) I do.

Correct incorrect spellings in the following sentences.

11. The next survivors will be sent to the Sahara dessert with only the cloths on their backs.

12. The dog was to hyper to eat his biscuits at 3:00, but by 6:00 he was quiet calm.

13. His peace of cake is bigger then mine, but whose keeping track?

14. Its not half passed two yet, is it?

15. The principal told me to stay after school for detention yesterday, but I choose not to.

16. I advise you not to take her advice.

17. Homework has an adverse affect on her social life.

18. They are all ready to go already.

19. The clothes she is wearing were made in Italy.

20. He was never conscience that the weather effected him so grately.

21. I don't want to get into an arguement with you.

22. That ride was absolutly exilarating.

23. Have you had you're innoculation for the flu virus yet?

24. Its time to seperate the men from the boys.

25. His authority supercedes that of all the other commanders.

26. They desided to leave the game for awhile and come back later.

27. Did we tell you about the strange occurence that we witnessed last night?

28. You had better book your accommodations early because the hotels are all ready filling up fast.

29. What advise do you have about which coarses I should take next semester?

30. All that is neccessary is that you bring a helmet and pads to the skate park.

Add –ing to the following words **according to the rules for doubling the last consonant.**

1. shoot	2. edit
3. grab	4. bawl
5. complain	6. ransom
7. run	8. tower
9. refer	10. travel

Key to Practice Quiz #2 on Spelling

Circle the correct word in parentheses.

1. Everyone appreciates a (complement, **compliment**) once in a while.

2. My house payment includes only forty dollars of the (**principal**, principle)

3. No one likes a (**deserter**, desserter).

4. Our state is having a difficult time (**choosing**, chosing) its electors.

5. That man is having a strange (affect, **effect**) on me.

6. Are you (**all ready**, already) to go?

7. Kalina loves school (accept, **except**) when she has to take a test.

8. (Its, **It's**) important to distinguish between love and pity.

9. He (lead, **led**) in popular votes, but she acquired the electors.

10. Torina spends more time socializing (**than**, then) I do.

Correct incorrect spellings in the following sentences.

11. The next survivors will be sent to the Sahara **desert** with only the **clothes** on their backs.

12. The dog was **too** hyper to eat his biscuits at 3:00, but by 6:00 he was **quite** calm.

13. His **piece** of cake is bigger **than** mine, but **who's** keeping track?

14. **It's** not half **past** two yet, is it?

15. The principal told me to stay after school for detention yesterday, but I **chose** not to.

16. I advise you not to take her advice.

17. Homework has an adverse **effect** on her social life.

18. They are all ready to go already.

19. The clothes she is wearing were made in Italy.

20. He was never **conscious** that the weather **affected** him so **greatly**.

21. I don't want to get into an argument with you.

22. That ride was absolutely exhilarating.

23. Have you had your inoculation for the flu virus yet?

24. It's time to separate the men from the boys.

25. His authority supersedes that of all the other commanders.

26. They decided to leave the game for a while and come back later.

27. Did we tell you about the strange occurrence that we witnessed last night?

28. You had better book your accommodations early because the hotels are already filling up fast.

29. What advice do you have about which courses I should take next semester?

30. All that is necessary is that you bring a helmet and pads to the skate park.

Add –ing to the following words **according to the rules for doubling the last consonant.**

1. shooting	6. editing
2. grabbing	7. bawling
3. complaining	8. ransoming
4. running	9. towering
5. referring	10. traveling

Practice Quiz #3 on Spelling

Correct all mispellings.

1. Yesterday I choose to sleep late instead of going to class.

2. Some people think the desert is beautiful, but I perfer the mountains.

3. I except your apolegy.

4. We are already to go to the party.

5. Please help you're self to a complimentary glass of wine.

6. She was not conscience of the man following closed behind her.

7. You may deduct the intrest but not the principle on your lone.

8. I don't know weather his comming to are party or not.

9. The team is highly skilled, but it lacks morale.

10. The conducter lead the orchestra.

11. The dog is chaseing it's tail.

12. Don't loose track of time.

13. This is the forth time I've come to Mexico.

14. Kane is the person whose tring to get a date with Maggie.

15. You should use passed tense in this sentence.

16. Lets wait for Tim and Troy; their always alot of fun.

17. I ate to many chips before supper.

18. It's later then you think.

19. Your going to like this grade.

20. Smokeing effects not only you but those around you.

Add –ing to the following words **according to the rules for doubling the last consonant**.

1. bask

2. permit

3. counsel

4. endeavor

5. total

6. join

7. put

8. sweep

9. commit

10. swim

Key to Practice Quiz #3 on Spelling

Correct all misspellings.

1. Yesterday I chose to sleep late instead of going to class.

2. Some people think the desert is beautiful, but I prefer the mountains.

3. I accept your apology.

4. We are all ready to go to the party.

5. Please help yourself to a complimentary glass of wine.

6. She was not conscious of the man following close behind her.

7. You may deduct the interest but not the principal on your loan.

8. I don't know whether he's coming to our party or not.

9. The team is highly skilled, but it lacks morale.

10. The conductor led the orchestra.

11. The dog is chasing its tail.

12. Don't lose track of time.

13. This is the fourth time I've come to Mexico.

14. Kane is the person who's trying to get a date with Maggie.

15. You should use past tense in this sentence.

16. Let's wait for Tim and Troy; they're always a lot of fun.

17. I ate too many chips before supper.

18. It's later than you think.

19. You're going to like this grade.

20. Smoking affects not only you but those around you.

Add –ing to the following words **according to the rules for doubling the last consonant**.

1. basking

2. permitting

3. counseling

4. endeavoring

5. totaling

6. joining

7. putting

8. sweeping

9. committing

10. swimming

Practice Quiz on Possessives, Plurals, and Contractions

Form contractions or possessives above the words in brackets, and **insert** apostrophes wherever necessary to words in the rest of the sentence.

Example:
         It's   your   cat's

Example: [It] about time [you] tax refund arrived; now we can have the cats teeth fixed.

1. [We] going to see which items have been taken to [they] new location.

2. [You] pass expires when [they] records show that you have visited the exhibit three times.

3. [They] the kind [who] parents are always busy.

4. The players costumes will be fitted in [they] dressing rooms.

5. [It] [me] CD, not [you].

6. The girls program should not run longer than an hour; each of [they] routines is only five minutes long, and [they] all ready to go.

7. One should never forget ones beginnings.

8. I shall call to tell them [who] coming.

9. Someones umbrella was left behind.

10. The pastors sermon stirred the parishioners to put lots of money into the collection basket.

11. This is [you] last chance to let her know [who] boss.

12. Its no surprise that Kaleb is jealous of [you] accomplishments.

13. The phones ringing every five minutes is making [I] headache worse.

14. [You] laptop may get too warm unless you ventilate its bottom.

15. I thought that this book was [you], but apparently it is [she].

Key to Practice Quiz on Possessives, Plurals, and Contractions

1. [We're] going to see which items have been taken to [their] new location.

2. [Your] pass expires when [their] records show that you have visited the exhibit three times.

3. [They're] the kind [whose] parents are always busy.

4. The players' costumes will be fitted in [their] dressing rooms.

5. [It's] [my] CD, not [yours].

6. The girls' program should not run longer than an hour; each of [their] routines is only five minutes long, and [they're] all ready to go.

7. One should never forget one's beginnings.

8. I shall call to tell them [who's] coming.

9. Someone's umbrella was left behind.

10. The pastor's sermon stirred the parishioners to put lots of money into the collection basket.

11. This is [your] last chance to let her know [who's] boss.

12. It's no surprise that Kaleb is jealous of [your] accomplishments.

13. The phone's ringing every five minutes is making [my] headache worse.

14. [Your] laptop may get too warm unless you ventilate its bottom.

15. I thought that this book was [yours], but apparently it is [hers].

Practice Quiz on Commas with Rules

Rule #1 - Commas **belong** before the coordinating conjunction (and, or, nor, but, for, so, yet) which joins two independent clauses.

Rule #2 - Commas **belong** after an introductory adverb clause.

Rule #3 - Commas **must not** separate other compound structures (two of the same grammatical structure).

Rule #4 – Commas **must not** separate main sentence elements (subject, predicate, direct object, complement).

Put commas where they belong in the following sentences, and write the number of the rule which applies **for each sentence** in the blank.

____ 1. We lost our oars and that was the end of our boating.

____ 2. We may leave Friday or we may wait until Monday.

____ 3. I wanted to go but could not get my car started.

____ 4. When I get to the sad part of a story I always cry.

____ 5. The truck was low on fuel but Jan made it to the next gas station.

____ 6. We couldn't cook dinner without electricity nor could we do our homework.

____ 7. No one really expected her to come but she was the first one there.

____ 8. What we need is stricter law enforcement.

____ 9. Because he was so determined to succeed Clement worked far into the night on his studies.

____10. Many people want what they don't need and need what they don't want.

____11. Even though he doesn't always like writing he enjoys having written.

____12. While they are in college they don't have much time for cooking.

____13. They asked the policeman whether they could park inside the grounds.

____14. She clipped her ice pick to her belt and slung her pack on her back.

____15. We wanted to attend the lecture by Amy Tan but we couldn't get tickets.

____16. The reason for the delay is that our computers were down.

___17. Whenever he is not sure of the spelling of a word he checks the dictionary because spell check is not always reliable.

___18. As they entered the door blew shut.

___19. Since it was the beginning of the semester there were no papers to write.

___20. You can go or stay.

Key to Practice Quiz on Commas with Rules

Rule #1 - Commas **belong** before the coordinating conjunction (and, or, nor, but, for, so, yet) which joins two independent clauses.

Rule #2 - Commas **belong** after an introductory adverb clause.

Rule #3 - Commas **must not** separate other compound structures (two of the same grammatical structure).

Rule #4 – Commas **must not** separate main sentence elements (subject, predicate, direct object, complement).

Put commas where they belong in the following sentences, and write the number of the rule which applies **for each sentence** in the blank.

_1_ 1. We lost our oars, and that was the end of our boating.

_1_ 2. We may leave Friday, or we may wait until Monday.

_3_ 3. I wanted to go but could not get my car started.

_2_ 4. When I get to the sad part of a story, I always cry.

_1_ 5. The truck was low on fuel, but he made it to the next gas station.

_1_ 6. We couldn't cook dinner without electricity, nor could we do our homework.

_1_ 7. No one really expected her to come, but she was the first one there.

_4_ 8. What we need is stricter law enforcement.

_2_ 9. Because he was so determined to succeed, Clement worked far into the night on his studies.

_3_ 10. Many people want what they don't need and need what they don't want.

_2_ 11. Even though he doesn't always like writing, he enjoys having written.

_2_ 12. While they are in college, they don't have much time for cooking.

_4_ 13. They asked the policeman whether they could park inside the grounds.

_3_ 14. She clipped her ice pick to her belt and slung her pack on her back.

_1_ 15. We wanted to attend the lecture by Amy Tan, but we couldn't get tickets.

_4_ 16. The reason for the delay is that our computers were down.

_2_ 17. Whenever he is not sure of the spelling of a word, he checks the dictionary because spell check is not always reliable.

_2_ 18. As they entered, the door blew shut.

_2_ 19. Since it was the beginning of the semester, there were no papers to write.

_3_ 20. You can go or stay.

Practice Quiz #1 with Commas and Semicolons

Correct the punctuation by adding commas or semi-colons where necessary. Do not change any wording. Some sentences are correct.

1. E. B. White's essay "Once More to the Lake" is a classic and many generations of readers have enjoyed it.

2. White writes about his childhood trips to the lake, and he compares them with taking his own son to the lake.

3. White notes changes in the vacation experience however he finds its essence is unchanged.

4. White describes the arrival, his room, and the other vacationers, but his focus is on the feelings these details evoke.

5. Concrete and specific details fill the essay its theme is an abstraction, the sense of mortality.

6. Some families enjoy vacationing at a lake others prefer to go to an ocean beach.

7. Carol's family vacations by camping or they may hike in a national park.

8. On her vacation, Natasha went to Santa Fe New Mexico consequently she was able to attend both the Santa Fe Opera and the Santa Fe Chamber Music Festival.

9. Native Americans live in the pueblo in Taos, New Mexico they worship in the pueblo's ancient church.

10. The Amish of Pennsylvania retain their old traditions; therefore, they do not drive cars.

11. The people whom we invited along are Kathy, my niece, Rick, her boyfriend, and Danica, his little sister.

12. Shiela wants to bake a peach pie for her new neighbors but first she will have to borrow a pie plate from them.

13. Jo Jo did not cover her hair before painting the garage consequently her coiffure will be spotted until the paint spatters brush out.

14. The CEO of the company which Jackson works for has a gambling problem he really needs to enter a treatment program or the entire company could go bankrupt.

15. When he arrives tell him I am too ill to go out.

16. The traffic on the interstate may be heavy but at least it is moving along if we had taken the back roads we would still be in Dane county.

17. Not long ago Jamie was struggling to keep up in her studies now she is at the top of her class because she attended a time management workshop.

18. When Dan and Lee bought their new boat they had no idea that it would end up to be a hole in the water into which they would pour money.

19. The golf tournament was a complete success even though the weather was somewhat uncooperative.

20. Greg is helping me make out my will I never realized how many possible situations there are to consider.

Key to Practice Quiz #1 with Commas and Semicolons

Correct the punctuation by adding commas or semi-colons where necessary. Do not change any wording. Some sentences are correct.

1. E. B. White's essay "Once More to the Lake" is a classic, and many generations of readers have enjoyed it.

2. White writes about his childhood trips to the lake, and he compares them with taking his own son to the lake.

3. White notes changes in the vacation experience; however, he finds its essence is unchanged.

4. White describes the arrival, his room, and the other vacationers; but his focus is on the feelings these details evoke.

5. Concrete and specific details fill the essay; its theme is an abstraction, the sense of mortality.

6. Some families enjoy vacationing at a lake; others prefer to go to an ocean beach.

7. Carol's family vacations by camping, or they may hike in a national park.

8. On her vacation, Natasha went to Santa Fe, New Mexico; consequently, she was able to attend both the Santa Fe Opera and the Santa Fe Chamber Music Festival.

9. Native Americans live in the pueblo in Taos, New Mexico; they worship in the pueblo's ancient church.

10. The Amish of Pennsylvania retain their old traditions; therefore, they do not drive cars.

11. The people whom we invited along are Kathy, my niece; Rick, her boyfriend; and Danica, his little sister.

12. Shiela wants to bake a peach pie for her new neighbors, but first she will have to borrow a pie plate from them.

13. Jo Jo did not cover her hair before painting the garage; consequently, her coiffure will be spotted until the paint spatters brush out.

14. The CEO of the company which Jackson works for has a gambling problem; he really needs to enter a treatment program, or the entire company could go bankrupt.

15. When he arrives, tell him I am too ill to go out.

16. The traffic on the interstate may be heavy, but at least it is moving along; if we had taken the back roads, we would still be in Dane county.

17. Not long ago Jamie was struggling to keep up in her studies; now she is at the top of her class because she attended a time management workshop.

18. When Dan and Lee bought their new boat, they had no idea that it would end up to be a hole in the water into which they would pour money.

19. The golf tournament was a complete success even though the weather was somewhat uncooperative.

20. Greg is helping me make out my will; I never realized how many possible situations there are to consider.

Practice Quiz #2 with Commas and Semicolons

1. I'm sure however that he will be here on time.

2. We just got back from Reno Nevada and it was tons of fun.

3. *The Bell Jar* by Sylvia Plath is a celebrated though disturbing book.

4. I know that your case is important therefore I will hear it first thing on Monday.

5. After work he plans to eat dinner watch some TV and do grammar exercises.

6. He picked up the roses bought the wine and drove two hours to meet her.

7. Tim Duncan who played basketball for the Spurs injured his knee.

8. However hard the guy tried he could not meet her needs in life.

9. I may see her this weekend or I may never see her again.

10. Cassie was born on April 6 1978 at St. Joseph's Hospital in Milwaukee Wisconsin.

11. The doctors realized that she had an irregular heartbeat and they placed her in the intensive care unit.

12. Her doctor told her parents that she would outgrow her heart condition in six months however this problem plagued her until she was a sophomore in high school.

13. Her condition supra-ventricular tachycardia triggered her heart to beat unusually fast and caused her to experience shortness of breath fatigue and the feeling that her heart was in her throat.

14. When she decided that she could not live with the condition any longer she decided to go through a procedure called a radio-frequency ablation to rid herself of this problem forever.

15. I am not one to gossip but I know something about him that I think you should know.

16. If it were a different situation I would behave differently.

17. Xiong Thao was born in Huntsville Kentucky on December 32 1986 and raised in Gulf Shores Alabama.

18. I think Josh that you eat too much junk food.

19. That car which had been in a bad wreck was repaired at Holden's Body Shop.

20. He is not graduating in May and his parents are not happy.

21. Sally the head cheerleader always wears a white sweater black pants and thick-soled shoes on game days.

22. To give shelter to lost animals is very generous.

23. "To be or not to be that is the question."

24. William Everson who was a poet and a printer died I believe four years ago.

25. I like my new apartment however it is small and my bed couch and chair take up too much room.

Key to Practice Quiz #2 with Commas and Semicolons

1. I'm sure, however, that he will be here on time.

2. We just got back from Reno, Nevada, and it was tons of fun.

3. *The Bell Jar*, by Sylvia Plath, is a celebrated, though disturbing, book.

4. I know that your case is important; therefore, I will hear it first thing on Monday.

5. After work he plans to eat dinner, watch some TV, and do grammar exercises.

6. That car, which had been in a bad wreck, was repaired at Holden's Body Shop.

7. If it were a different situation, I would behave differently.

8. However hard the guy tried, he could not meet her needs in life.

9. I may see her this weekend, or I may never see her again.

10. Cassie was born on April 6, 1978, at St. Joseph's Hospital in Milwaukee, Wisconsin.

11. The doctors realized that she had an irregular heartbeat, and they placed her in the intensive care unit.

12. Her doctor told her parents that she would outgrow her heart condition in six months; however, this problem plagued her until she was a sophomore in high school.

13. Her condition, supra-ventricular tachycardia, triggered her heart to beat unusually fast and caused her to experience shortness of breath, fatigue, and the feeling that her heart was in her throat.

14. When she decided that she could not live with the condition any longer, she decided to go through a procedure called a radio-frequency ablation to rid herself of this problem forever.

15. I am not one to gossip, but I know something about him that I think you should know.

16. Tim Duncan, who played basketball for the Spurs, injured his knee.

17. Xiong Thao was born in Huntsville, Kentucky, on December 32, 1986, and raised in Gulf Shores, Alabama.

18. I think, Josh, that you eat too much junk food.

19. He picked up the roses, bought the wine, and drove two hours to meet her.

20. He is not graduating in May, and his parents are not happy.

21. Sally, the head cheerleader, always wears a white sweater, black pants, and thick-soled shoes on game days.

22. To give shelter to lost animals is very generous.

23. "To be or not to be; that is the question."

24. William Everson, who was a poet and a printer, died, I believe, four years ago.

25. I like my new apartment; however, it is small, and my bed, couch, and chair take up too much room.

Practice Quiz #1 on Spelling and Punctuation

Insert proper punctuation, and change spelling where neccesary. Indicate italics by underlining. Do not change capitolization.

1. Shes going to the stores reopening with her sons

2. The title of Achebe's first novel Things Fall Apart comes from a line in the poem The Second Coming by W B Yeats

3. Jon was our class valedictorian nevertheless he is still looking for a job

4. James house is the nicest of all our friends

5. The book is theirs but they said theyd share it if we promise not to right on its pages

6. The Jones flowers are absolutely beautifull

7. His sins are those of lust, theirs are those of gluttany

8. Fellinis films are inferior to Bergmans, though niether matchs the films of Truffaut

9. She liked all her students; even the ones who didnt do there homework on time

10. She had never moped a floor in her life but she was willing to try

11. Angelas dress wont be ready in time because the two girls mothers who said theyd help so it have been out of town

12. Do you want to go to the movies asked Anne

13. I read Robert Frosts poem, After Apple Picking

14. Your the only person here who likes cold whether

15. Dont you want to go sking with the Smiths

16. The short story, The Bear, can be found in many books including The Collected Works of William Faulkner

17. Is that soda yours or your roomates

18. Wasn't yesterday fun Candy asked Bambi her friend as they walked to dinner

19. Did you remember to invite Jill Rebecca and Lisa

20. I invited the following people Mike Roger Bill Frank and Ed

21. I didnt invite Mark he was being a jerk today

22. What is the plot of Poes narrative poem The Raven.

23. When I read my paper aloud I always catch some careless errors

24. The chicken crossed the road for the following reasons to find something for dinner to get out of the sun and to see a new prospective on life

25. We couldn't do the decorating without a stepladder nor could we mow the lawn without a mower

Key to Practice Quiz #1 on Spelling and Punctuation

Insert proper punctuation, and change spelling where necessary. Indicate italics by underlining. Do not change capitalization.

1. She's going to the store's reopening with her sons.

2. The title of Achebe's first novel, *Things Fall Apart*, comes from a line in the poem "The Second Coming," by W. B. Yeats.

3. Jon was our class valedictorian; nevertheless, he is still looking for a job.

4. James' house is the nicest of all our friends'.

5. The book is theirs, but they said they'd share it if we promise not to write on its pages.

6. The Jones' flowers are absolutely beautiful.

7. His sins are those of lust; theirs are those of gluttony.

8. Fellini's films are inferior to Bergman's though neither's match the films of Truffaut.

9. She liked all her students, even the ones who didn't do their homework on time.

10. She had never mopped a floor in her life, but she was willing to try.

11. Angela's dress won't be ready in time because the two girls' mothers, who said they'd help sew it, have been out of town.

12. "Do you want to go to the movies?" asked Anne.

13. I read Robert Frost's poem "After Apple Picking."

14. You're the only person here who likes cold weather.

15. Don't you want to go skiing with the Smiths?

16. The short story "The Bear" can be found in many books, including *The Collected Works* of William Faulkner.

17. Is that soda yours or your roommate's?

18. "Wasn't yesterday fun?" Candy asked Bambi, her friend, as they walked to dinner.

19. Did you remember to invite Jill, Rebecca, and Lisa?

20. I invited the following people: Mike, Roger, Bill, Frank, and Ed.

21. I didn't invite Mark; he was being a jerk today.

22. What is the plot of Poe's narrative poem "The Raven"?

23. When I read my paper aloud, I always catch some careless errors.

24. The chicken crossed the road for the following reasons: to find something for dinner, to get out of the sun, and to see a new perspective on life.

25. We couldn't do the decorating without a stepladder, nor could we mow the lawn without a mower.

Practice Quiz #2 on Spelling and Punctuation

Insert periods, question marks, exclamation marks, colons, apostrophes, semicolons, and commas where appropriate. Indicate where italics are necessary by underlining. Do not change capitalization. Correct spelling errors.

1. I dont know what to say Im too tired to think

2. Ive given up trying to match clothes with accesories brown shoes black coat brown perse

3. Feel free to go whenever you like said the building manager

4. No said Amy Im waiting for Cory Hes coming to pick me up

5. Where did you here about this postion

6. I saw an intresting add in the La Crosse Tribune yesterday said June

7. Do you want to go downtown tonight asked Julie

8. Have you read the poem Lenore by Edgar Allan Poe

9. Have you wached the movie Ferris Buehlers Day Off

10. The short story Wants by Grace Paley contains more then one narative

11. I wish the sun would come out then I could go to the beach for the afternoon

12. I want him to be more like his brother his brother is a wonderfull student and he is all ways on time

13. Jessica Tommys little sister walked to school

14. She was with Karen a second grader Kevin a third grader and her nieghbor Jenny

15. They use to ride the bus but it broke down last week

16. Having forgotten to set her alarm she caused all of them to arrive late however the teacher was not mad

17. Because she goes to bed late getting out of bed is a difficult task this pozes a problem

18. Jimmy bought a new computer but had trouble transfering his old programs to it.

Key to Practice Quiz #2 on Spelling and Punctuation

Insert periods, question marks, exclamation marks, colons, apostrophes, semi colons, and commas where appropriate. Indicate where italics are necessary by underlining. Do not change capitalization. Correct spelling errors.

1. I don't know what to say; I'm too tired to think.

2. I've given up trying to match clothes with accessories: brown shoes, black coat, brown purse.

3. "Feel free to go whenever you like," said the building manager.

4. "No," said Amy. "I'm waiting for Cory. He's coming to pick me up."

5. Where did you hear about this position?

6. "I saw an interesting ad in the *Chicago Tribune* yesterday," said June.

7. "Do you want to go downtown tonight?" asked Julie.

8. Have you read the poem "Lenore," by Edgar Allan Poe?

9. Have you watched the movie Ferris Buehler's Day Off?

10. The short story "Wants," by Grace Paley, contains more than one narrative.

11. I wish the sun would come out; then I could go to the beach for the afternoon.

12. I want him to be more like his brother; his brother is a wonderful student, and he is always on time.

13. Jessica, Tommy's little sister, walked to school.

14. She was with Karen, a second grader; Kevin, a third grader; and her neighbor, Jenny.

15. They used to ride the bus, but it broke down last week.

16. Having forgotten to set her alarm, she caused all of them to arrive late; however, the teacher was not mad.

17. Because she goes to bed late, getting out of bed is a difficult task; this poses a problem.

18. Jimmy bought a new computer but had trouble transferring his old programs to it.

Practice Quiz on Adjectives and Adverbs

Choose the correct form in parentheses and draw an arrow to the word that it modifies, or correct comparative and superlative usage.

1. This house smells really (bad, badly).

2. She plays soccer very (good, well).

3. The (terrible, terribly) dressed man went to a fancy restaurant and got kicked out.

4. I feel really (happy, happily) because school is over soon.

5. She is walking (slow, slowly), and that is why she will be late for the meeting.

6. My arm hurts (bad, badly).

7. The woman sang (bold, boldly).

8. The meal we had at Julie's was (good, well).

9. I feel (perfect, perfectly) fine driving in the dark.

10. My mother has an (unusual, unusually) way of washing the dishes.

11. The rain beat (soft, softly) against the window.

12. The water heated (extremely, extreme) fast.

13. She was (wrong, wrongly) accused of cheating.

14. They lived (happily, happy) ever after.

15. She sprinted (quickly, quick) across the busy street.

16. The cafeteria serves the baddest food.

17. That dog is the most ugly I have ever seen.

18. What is worst than bad milk?

19. Diet Coke is the better of the three brands.

20. Her wedding was the most best day of all.

Key to Practice Quiz on Adjectives and Adverbs

Choose the correct form in parentheses and draw an arrow to the word that it modifies, or correct comparative and superlative usage.

1. This house smells really (bad, badly).

2. She plays soccer very (good, well).

3. The (terrible, terribly) dressed man went to a fancy restaurant and got kicked out.

4. I feel really (happy, happily) because school is over soon.

5. She is walking (slow, slowly), and that is why she will be late for the meeting.

6. My arm hurts (bad, badly).

7. The woman sang (bold, boldly).

8. The meal we had at Julie's was (good, well).

9. I feel (perfect, perfectly) fine driving in the dark.

10. My mother has an (unusual, unusually) way of washing the dishes.

11. The rain beat (soft, softly) against the window.

12. The water heated (extremely, extreme) fast.

13. She was (wrong, wrongly) accused of cheating.

14. They lived (happily, happy) ever after.

15. She sprinted (quickly, quick) across the busy street.

16. The cafeteria serves the worst food.

17. That dog is the ugliest I have ever seen.

18. What is worse than bad milk?

19. Diet Coke is the better of the two brands.

20. Her wedding was the best day of all.

Practice Quiz #1 on Agreement

Underline the subject and choose the correct corresponding verb.

1. One of my friends (has, have) been offered a trip to Walt Disney World.

2. Anyone who (was, were) at the show saw a fantastic performance.

3. I (hope, hoped) you (is, are) well enough to go to work on Friday.

4. Each of the dogs (was, were) fed in (his, their) own dish.

5. (We, Us) have made a decision; we (want, wants) to go to the city tonight for dinner and dancing by moonlight.

6. (Doesn't, Don't) he realize that we (is, are) running out of time and money?

7. I (wonder, wondered) if he is ever going to get his act together.

8. The conditions of my agreement (has, have) changed a little, and I (hope, hoped) that I will be able to go through with it.

9. She (is, was) going to the store tomorrow, but (me, I) think she (is, was) going to stay home.

10. Most of the flowers (grows, grow) beautifully, but some of them (wilt, wilts) right away.

11. Most of the art (display, displays) impressionistic influences.

12. Most of the artworks (display, displays) postmodern flourishes as well.

13. The Ataris (is, are) a good band, but Screeching Weasel (is, are) a great band.

14. Everyone (votes, vote) for his or her favorite candidate.

15. None of the pride I feel (is, are) from winning.

16. (They, Them) on the committee have quite a bit of power at their disposal.

17. (Have, Has) each of you picked out which cookie cutters you want to use?

18. If (they, them) would simply choose a direction, their destination would reach (they, them) sooner.

19. Several of the candies (was, were) crushed in the bag, but neither Jessie nor her sisters (was, were) to blame.

20. When one completes (his, her, his or her, their) homework, (he, she, he or she, they) may go to lunch.

21. All of the children (have, has) been watching (his, her, his or her, their) favorite TV programs after school instead of doing (his, her, his or her, their) homework.

22. Everybody is making (himself, herself, himself or herself, themselves) a sandwich at the picnic, but neither the employees nor the boss (know, knows) who will pay for the food.

23. He (don't, doesn't) understand the math problem.

24. I often wonder if we (is, are) truly alone in the universe.

25. (Wasn't, Weren't) you the one who asked for my phone number?

26. It (doesn't, don't) seem like many students are motivated this time of year.

27. Do you know if Jake (is, are) coming tomorrow?

28. Each of us (wish, wishes) the school year was over.

29. Both Jason and Julie (is, are) attending UNLV.

30. (Was, Were) the concert last night?

31. One of my sisters (has, have) three sons.

32. Most of the animals (was, were) asleep by ten.

33. Leslie and I (is, are) going to the mall.

34. Neither Jan nor her eight sisters (is, are) going to the mall.

35. One of the papers (look, looks) like he spilled something on it.

Key to Practice Quiz #1 on Agreement

1. One has been offered

2. who was

3. I hope   you are

4. Each was fed in his

5. We have made; we want

6. Doesn't he realize   we are running

7. I wonder   he is going

8. conditions have changed   I hope

9. She was going   I think   she is going

10. Most grow   some wilt

11. Most displays

12. Most display

13. Ataris are   Screeching Weasel is

14. Everyone votes

15. None is

16. They have

17. Has each picked

18. they would choose   destination would reach them

19. Several were crushed   neither Jessie nor her sisters were

20. one completes (his, her, his or her) homework, (he, she, he or she)

21. All have been watching their   their

22. Everybody is making (himself, herself, himself or herself)   neither the
employees nor the boss knows

23. He doesn't understand

24. we are

25. Weren't you

26. It doesn't seem

27. Jake is coming

28. Each wishes

29. Jason and Julie are attending

30. Was the concert

31. One has

32. Most were

33. Leslie and I are going

34. Neither Jan nor her eight sisters are going

35. One looks

36. None is

Practice Quiz #2 on Agreement

Underline the subject and choose the correct corresponding verb.

1. The photographs taken for the cooking magazine (looks, look) good enough to eat.

2. Rivulets of dew (covers, cover) the canvas top of my sleeping bag.

3. A train with both coaches and sleeping cars (leaves, leave) at eleven o'clock.

4. Runners in the last race (competes, compete) for a gold cup.

5. Studying the abnormalities in this specimen (helps, help) us to advance our theory.

6. Blood samples taken from the patient (confirms, confirm) the doctor's diagnosis.

7. The five-day conference, attended by leading scientists and public officials, (is, are) sponsored by several professional societies.

8. One computer for two or more students (seems, seem) inadequate.

9. Weather conditions in the valley (surprises, surprise) some visitors.

10. Her arguments against the plan (convinces, convince) me.

11. Warm, moist air flowing in from the oceans (brings, bring) heavy rains.

12. The effects of radiation on the human body (concerns, concern) the average citizen as well as the scientist.

13. A plane with sixty-five passengers aboard (is, are) scheduled to take off in three hours.

14. Large amounts of milk (comes, come) into the city every day.

15. An infant's need for long naps and frequent feedings (does, do) make a big difference in the average household.

16. Huge billboards on every road for miles around (tells, tell) the traveler that he is approaching Milltown.

17. The metal alloys used in a modern jet plane (meets, meet) rigid standards of quality.

18. The ringing sound of footsteps on stone pavements always (reminds, remind) me of my first visit to the shopping district downtown.

19. The last match of the semifinals (is, are) now going on.

20. The old conflict between central authority and states' rights (has, have) never been completely solved in any country.

21. Neither of these arguments (convinces, convince) me.

22. Most of the voters in the district (is, are) Democrats.

23. One of the things we like most about the new cars (is, are) the wide choice of colors.

24. After a heavy lunch few of the team (seems, seem) quite ready for a practice session.

25. The student in charge of the awards (does, do) not choose the winners.

26. Many of the good things in life (arrives, arrive) unexpectedly.

27. After the floods one of the first and most pressing tasks (was, were) to care for thousands of homeless people.

28. Each of the books we will receive (contains, contain) facts that we must know.

29. All of the commuters, like a solid wave of men and women, (pours, pour) down the stairs and into the train.

30. (Does, Do) everyone on both teams know the rules of the game?

31. Every one of the communities under discussion (has, have) adequate school facilities.

32. Some of the items on the menu (looks, look) like a French lesson.

33. One of the pictures (shows, show) all nine members of the team gathered around home plate.

34. Neither the senior team nor the alumni team (is, are) our chief threat.

35. Everybody working on these problems (faces, face) the same obstacles.

36. During the winter months the road linking the three towns (has, have) always been closed.

37. A code message, accompanied by maps and other papers, (was, were) delivered to all officers just before the battle.

38. Our planet, like all the other members of the solar system, (follows, follow) an orbit around the sun.

39. Jagged, uneven rocks, as well as the slippery coating of ice, (make, makes) the path difficult to follow.

40. His straightforward and powerful speech in defense of his policies (appears, appear) to have carried the day.

41. Several members of the Italian club, along with Ms. Robinson, their faculty advisor, (is, are) to speak at the meeting.

42. The forces of each of the two teams (is, are) evenly matched.

43. My class notes, like yours, (does, do) not agree with the textbook in every detail.

44. The trouble with many speeches, accusations, and television appearances in an election year (is, are) that they confuse rather than clarify the issues.

45. Layers of foam rubber under the motor (cushions, cushion) its vibration.

Key to Practice Quiz #2 on Agreement

Underline the subject and choose the correct corresponding verb.

1. The photographs taken for the cooking magazine (looks, look) good enough to eat.

2. Rivulets of dew (covers, cover) the canvas top of my sleeping bag.

3. A train with both coaches and sleeping cars (leaves, leave) at eleven o'clock.

4. Runners in the last race (competes, compete) for a gold cup.

5. Studying the abnormalities in this specimen (helps, help) us to advance our theory.

6. Blood samples taken from the patient (confirms, confirm) the doctor's diagnosis.

7. The five-day conference, attended by leading scientists and public officials, (is, are) sponsored by several professional societies.

8. One computer for two or more students (seems, seem) inadequate.

9. Weather conditions in the valley (surprises, surprise) some visitors.

10. Her arguments against the plan (convinces, convince) me.

11. Warm, moist air flowing in from the oceans (brings, bring) heavy rains.

12. The effects of radiation on the human body (concerns, concern) the average citizen as well as the scientist.

13. A plane with sixty-five passengers aboard (is, are) scheduled to take off in three hours.

14. Large amounts of milk (comes, come) into the city every day.

15. An infant's need for long naps and frequent feedings (does, do) make a big difference in the average household.

16. Huge billboards on every road for miles around (tells, tell) the traveler that he is approaching Milltown.

17. The metal alloys used in a modern jet plane (meets, meet) rigid standards of quality.

18. The ringing sound of footsteps on stone pavements always (reminds, remind) me of my first visit to the shopping district downtown.

19. The last match of the semifinals (is, are) now going on.

20. The old conflict between central authority and states' rights (has, have) never been completely solved in any country.

21. Neither of these arguments (convinces, convince) me.

22. Most of the voters in the district (is, are) Democrats.

23. One of the things we like most about the new cars (is, are) the wide choice of colors.

24. After a heavy lunch few of the team (seems, seem) quite ready for a practice session.

25. The student in charge of the awards (does, do) not choose the winners.

26. Many of the good things in life (arrives, arrive) unexpectedly.

27. After the floods one of the first and most pressing tasks (was, were) to care for thousands of homeless people.

28. Each of the books we will receive (contains, contain) facts that we must know.

29. <u>All</u> of the commuters, like a solid wave of men and women, (pours, <u>pour</u>) down the stairs and into the train.

30. (<u>Does</u>, Do) <u>everyone</u> on both teams know the rules of the game?

31. Every <u>one</u> of the communities under discussion (<u>has</u>, have) adequate school facilities.

32. <u>Some</u> of the items on the menu (looks, <u>look</u>) like a French lesson.

33. <u>One</u> of the pictures (<u>shows</u>, show) all nine members of the team gathered around home plate.

34. Neither the senior <u>team</u> nor the alumni <u>team</u> (<u>is</u>, are) our chief threat.

35. <u>Everybody</u> working on these problems (<u>faces</u>, face) the same obstacles.

36. During the winter months the <u>road</u> linking the three towns (<u>has</u>, have) always been closed.

37. A code <u>message</u>, accompanied by maps and other papers, (<u>was</u>, were) delivered to all officers just before the battle.

38. Our <u>planet</u>, like all the other members of the solar system, (<u>follows</u>, follow) an orbit around the sun.

39. Jagged, uneven <u>rocks</u>, as well as the slippery coating of ice, (<u>make</u>, makes) the path difficult to follow.

40. His straightforward and powerful <u>speech</u> in defense of his policies (<u>appears</u>, appear) to have carried the day.

41. Several <u>members</u> of the Italian club, along with Ms. Robinson, their faculty advisor, (is, <u>are</u>) to speak at the meeting.

42. The <u>forces</u> of each of the two teams (is, <u>are</u>) evenly matched.

43. My class <u>notes</u>, like yours, (does, <u>do</u>) not agree with the textbook in every detail.

44. The <u>trouble</u> with many speeches, accusations, and television appearances in an election year (<u>is</u>, are) that <u>they</u> confuse rather than clarify the issues.

45. <u>Layers</u> of foam rubber under the motor (cushions, <u>cushion</u>) its vibration.

Practice Quiz #3 on Agreement

Choose the proper pronoun and draw an arrow to its antecedent. Choose correct verb forms when appropriate.

Example: One of the children left (their, her) backpack on the playground.

1. The parents of a student with a learning disability should not immediately go running to (their, his or her) doctor asking for a prescription.

2. The logo for that company definitely suits (their, its) product line.

3. None of the dogs at the pet store (has, have) had (its, their) dew claws removed.

4. (Have, Has) any of them seen (his or her, their) test results yet?

5. Some from the crowd (is, are) slowly leaving the stadium.

6. Some of the crowd (is blocking, are blocking) the roadway.

7. Each of the customers (need, needs) to bring (his or her, their) coupons to the sale.

8. We are waiting until more of the people standing in line (have, has) passed through the gate and taken (their, his or her) (seats, seat).

9. How many of the foods (need, needs) to be put into (their, its) own (containers, container)?

10. Everyone in the room can easily see (themselves, himself or herself) in the situation that the pastor has described.

11. Each of the chairs (need, needs) to have (their, its) pad reupholstered.

12. Everyone who has taken this course will be thankful for all that (they, he or she) (have, has) learned.

13. (Are, Is) any of the items on your list going back to (their, its) original owner?

14. Every one of them (has, have) been summoned to search for the lost puppy.

Key to Practice Quiz #3 on Agreement

Choose the proper pronoun and draw an arrow to its antecedent. Choose correct verb forms when appropriate.

Example: One of the children left (their, **her**) backpack on the playground.

1. The parents of a student with a learning disability should not immediately go running to (their, **his or her**) doctor asking for a prescription. (It wouldn't make sense for the parents to go to their own doctor for their child's prescription.)

2. The logo for that company definitely suits (their, **its**) product line.

3. **None** of the dogs at the pet store (has, **have**) had (its, **their**) dew claws removed. (pl. because of dogs)

4. (**Have**, Has) **any** of them seen (his or her, **their**) test results yet? (pl. because of them)

5. **Some** from the crowd (is, **are**) slowly leaving the stadium. (pl. because the crowd is seen as individuals—some people from the crowd)

6. **Some** of the crowd (**is** blocking, are blocking) the roadway. (sing. because the crowd is seen as one entity—a portion of the crowd)

7. **Each** of the customers (need, **needs**) to bring (**his or her**, their) coupons to the sale.

8. We are waiting until **more** of the people standing in line (**have**, has) passed through the gate and taken (**their**, his or her) (**seats**, seat).

9. How **many** of the foods (**need**, needs) to be put into (**their**, its) own (**containers**, container)?

183

10. Everyone in the room can easily see (themselves, himself or herself) in the situation that the pastor has described.

11. Each of the chairs (need, needs) to have (their, its) pad reupholstered.

12. Everyone who has taken this course will be thankful for all that (they, he or she) (have, has) learned.

13. (Are, Is) any of the items on your list going back to (their, its) original owner? (pl. because of items)

14. Every one of them (has, have) been summoned to search for the lost puppy.

Practice Quiz #1 on Case

Besides choosing the proper form in parentheses, indicate whether the function of that pronoun is subject, sub; predicate noun, PN; direct object, do; indirect object, io; object of preposition, op; NP of infinitive, NPi; or NP of gerund, NPg.

1. My friend and (me, I) went to see a movie yesterday.

2. I am better than (she, her).

3. (You, Your) snoring drives me crazy.

4. She can hold her breath longer than (I, me).

5. They invited (we, us) to the party on Tuesday.

6. Give the ball to (whoever, whomever) can run the fastest.

7. Talla and (I, me) had a lot of fun at the mall this afternoon.

8. I scared (her, she) when I jumped out of the closet.

9. (We, Us) musicians have to stick together through the strike.

10. Did you give the keys to (he, him)?

11. Ben asked her and (I, me) to go to the store.

12. Every time they send (him, he) and (her, she) out, the two always get sidetracked.

13. I can run faster than (her, she).

14. If I were (her, she), I would buy the red car.

15. Colt and (he, him) went to the movie.

16. They left the house for John and (me, I) to clean.

17. (We, Us) women are going to the concert next week.

18. She left it up to (she, her) and (I, me) to decide.

19. I went with Tom and (he, him) to dinner.

20. Beth and (I, me) had a good time at the beach.

Key to Practice Quiz #1 on Case

Besides choosing the proper form in parentheses, indicate whether the function of that pronoun is subject, sub; predicate noun, PN; direct object, do; indirect object, io; object of preposition, op; NP of infinitive, NPi; or NP of gerund, NPg.

1. My friend and (me, I) went to see a movie yesterday. sub

2. I am better than (she, her). sub (she is)

3. (You, Your) snoring drives me crazy. NPg

4. She can hold her breath longer than (I, me). sub (I can)

5. They invited (we, us) to the party on Tuesday. do

6. Give the ball to (whoever, whomever) can run the fastest. sub (of can run)

7. Talla and (I, me) had a lot of fun at the mall this afternoon. sub

8. I scared (her, she) when I jumped out of the closet. do

9. (We, Us) musicians have to stick together through the strike. sub

10. Did you give the keys to (he, him)? op

11. Ben asked her and (I, me) to go to the store. NPi

12. Every time they send (him, he) and (her, she) out, the two always get sidetracked. do

13. I can run faster than (her, she). sub (she can run)

14. If I were (her, she), I would buy the red car. PN

15. Colt and (he, him) went to the movie. sub

16. They left the house for John and (me, I) to clean. NPi

17. (We, Us) women are going to the concert next week. sub

18. She left it up to (she, her) and (I, me) to decide. op

19. I went with Tom and (he, him) to dinner. op

20. Beth and (I, me) had a good time at the beach. sub

Practice Quiz #2 on Case

Besides choosing the proper form in parentheses, indicate whether the function of that pronoun is subject, sub; predicate noun, PN; direct object, do; indirect object, io; object of preposition, op; NP of infinitive, NPi; or NP of gerund, NPg.

1. I like Matt better than (he, him).

2. Give this to (whoever, whomever) gets here first.

3. You're supposed to chase (him, he) and (me, I).

4. Althea can paint a lot better than (her, she).

5. (Whom, Who) shall I make this check out to?

6. He said you would know (who, whom) should take this home.

7. (Him, His) winning the race changed my opinion of him.

8. His mother is worried about (him, his) driving too fast.

9. I don't care (who, whom) I baby sit.

10. (Who, Whom) should I say is calling?

11. We didn't do it; it was (they, them) over there.

12. There is no question about (who, whom) my candidate will be.

13. He is a man (who, whom) we all know and trust.

14. I wish I knew (who, whom) you were thinking of when you smiled a moment ago.

15. For students (who, whom) the faculty committee has chosen for special commendation, the graduation ceremonies are particularly exciting.

16. Will everyone (who, whom) you invited be able to come?

17. Among the last to be called were Hedda and (I, me).

18. You can probably handle this problem at least as well as (she, her).

19. Was it (he, him) (who, whom) the scholarship committee selected?

Key to Practice Quiz #2 on Case

Besides choosing the proper form in parentheses, indicate whether the function of that pronoun is subject, sub; predicate noun, PN; direct object, do; indirect object, io; object of preposition, op; NP of infinitive, NPi; or NP of gerund, NPg.

1. I like Matt better than (he, him). he if it means better than he likes Matt – sub; him if it means better than I like him - do

2. Give this to (whoever, whomever) gets here first. sub

3. You're supposed to chase (him, he) and (me, I). do

4. Althea can paint a lot better than (her, she). sub

5. (Whom, Who) shall I make this check out to? op

6. He said you would know (who, whom) should take this home. sub

7. (Him, His) winning the race changed my opinion of him. NPg

8. His mother is worried about (him, his) driving too fast. op

9. I don't care (who, whom) I baby sit. do

10. (Who, Whom) should I say is calling? sub (I should say who is calling)

11. We didn't do it; it was (they, them) over there. PN

12. There is no question about (who, whom) my candidate will be. PN

13. He is a man (who, whom) we all know and trust. do

14. I wish I knew (who, whom) you were thinking of when you smiled a moment ago. op

15. For students (who, whom) the faculty committee has chosen for special commendation, the graduation ceremonies are particularly exciting. do

16. Will everyone (who, whom) you invited be able to come? do

17. Among the last to be called were Hedda and (I, me). sub

18. You can probably handle this problem at least as well as (she, her). sub

19. Was it (he, him) (who, whom) the scholarship committee selected? PN do

Practice Quiz #3 on Case

Besides choosing the proper form in parentheses, indicate whether the function of that pronoun is subject, sub; predicate noun, PN; direct object, do; indirect object, io; object of preposition, op; NP of infinitive, NPi; or NP of gerund, NPg.

1. We will have to do without Susan and (he, him).
2. This is a good rule for (we, us) beginners.
3. Didn't anyone but Rick and (she, her) arrive on time?
4. To his assistants and (he, him) belongs the credit for making the dance a success.
5. For the curtain calls, stand beside Alex and (I, me).
6. Is there a game scheduled between our team and (they, them)?
7. Women like Jenna and (she, her) are always well groomed.
8. On his good days, Joe can play rings around Andy and (I, me).
9. Can we expect Kalle and (they, them) to help us when we need them?
10. Library privileges will be withheld from those (who, whom) have been found guilty of mutilating borrowed books.
11. Vote for the student (who, whom) has done most for the class.
12. It may be hard to pass judgment on someone (who, whom) has been a close friend since you entered school.
13. There is no question about (who, whom) my candidate will be.
14. He is a man (who, whom) we all know and trust.
15. Guess (who, whom) I met this morning?
16. The guy (who, whom) looked like the best swimmer turned out to be one of the worst.
17. The leader, obviously, should be someone (who, whom) the students already look to for guidance.
18. There can be no question about (who, whom) was the winner of that debate.
19. As an orator, she is a woman (who, whom) no one could accuse of using a few words where many will do.
20. This trophy will go to (whoever, whomever) wins the championship in three successive years.
21. If you know (who, whom) owns this book, please give it to her.
22. We may choose (whoever, whomever) we wish for our representative.
23. Mr. Ross, (who, whom) I had never even heard of before, turned out to be the best teacher I ever had.
24. Will everyone (who, whom) you invited be able to come?
25. These civil-defense volunteers must be people (who, whom) we can rely upon.

Key to Practice Quiz #3 on Case

Besides choosing the proper form in parentheses, indicate whether the function of that pronoun is subject, sub; predicate noun, PN; direct object, do; indirect object, io; object of preposition, op; NP of infinitive, NPi; or NP of gerund, NPg.

1. We will have to do without Susan and (he, **him**). op

2. This is a good rule for (we, **us**) beginners. op

3. Didn't anyone but Rick and (she, **her**) arrive on time? op (think of 'but' as the
preposition 'except')

4. To his assistants and (he, **him**) belongs the credit for making the dance a success.
op

5. For the curtain calls, stand beside Alex and (I, **me**). op

6. Is there a game scheduled between our team and (they, **them**)? op

7. Women like Jenna and (she, **her**) are always well groomed. op

8. On his good days, Joe can play rings around Andy and (I, **me**). op

9. Can we expect Kalle and (they, **them**) to help us when we need them? NPi

10. The leader, obviously, should be someone (who, **whom**) the students already look to for guidance. op

11. Vote for the student (**who**, whom) has done most for the class. sub

12. It may be hard to pass judgment on someone (**who**, whom) has been a close friend since you entered school. sub

13. There is no question about (**who**, whom) my candidate will be. PN

14. He is a man (who, **whom**) we all know and trust. do

15. Guess (who, **whom**) I met this morning? do

16. The guy (**who**, whom) looked like the best swimmer turned out to be one of the worst. sub

17. Library privileges will be withheld from those (**who**, whom) have been found guilty of mutilating borrowed books. sub

18. There can be no question about (**who**, whom) was the winner of that debate. sub

19. As an orator, she is a woman (who, **whom**) no one could accuse of using a few words where many will do. do

20. This trophy will go to (**whoever**, whomever) wins the championship in three successive years. sub

21. If you know (**who**, whom) owns this book, please give it to her. sub

22. We may choose (whoever, **whomever**) we wish for our representative. do

23. Mr. Ross, (who, **whom**) I had never even heard of before, turned out to be the best teacher I ever had. op

24. Will everyone (who, **whom**) you invited be able to come? do

25. These civil-defense volunteers must be people (who, **whom**) we can rely upon.
op

Practice Quiz on Dangling and Misplaced Modifiers

Rearrange parts of the sentence or rewrite it to eliminate dangling or misplaced modifiers.

1. After clearing off the table and putting the dishes away, the cat was let into the kitchen.

2. While looking at the store window, Stephanie's purse was snatched.

3. Thrashing about, I tried to wake my sister from her nightmare.

4. After getting out of the car and walking up the front steps to my house, my dog greeted me at the door.

5. I gave the movie to a friend that I didn't like too much.

6. After taking the test, the professor informed me that I failed.

7. Crawling across the carpet, I watched my baby niece, Alison, yesterday.

8. Climbing from tree to tree, Matt and I laughed at the squirrels.

9. After standing in line for five hours, the manager announced that all tickets were sold.

10. Having broken his hand, the nurse said he could not play basketball.

11. I will leave the money on the dresser that you can put in your pocket.

12. At the age of nine, my father had another child.

13. While playing soccer, Colton's peanut butter sandwich was stolen.

14. Being a funny speaker, I always attended her shows.

15. Twinkling in the night sky, I gazed at the stars.

16. After washing and waxing the floor, my dog slid across the room.

17. At the age of seven, my parents bought a new house.

18. I am going on a date with a guy who owns a scooter named Kade.

19. Flying through the air, I saw a kite.

20. After finishing a week's worth of homework, a beer would have been nice.

21. Tori left with a guy with a Mustang convertible named Cruz.

22. Diving through the sky, I ducked my head from the angry bird.

23. After studying for two hours, the grammar assignment went slowly.

24. Being snooty I couldn't stand to be near her.

25. After running three miles, taking a shower seemed like a good idea.

26. Taking her in his arms the moon hid behind a cloud.

27. Thoughtfully beginning to dress, the new blue jeans and clean shirt reminded him that at last he had a job.

28. Working really hard, the term paper was finished in six hours.

29. When ten years old my mother gave me a ring.

30. After asking three or four people, the right road was finally found.

31. After cleaning my room, my dog wanted to go for a walk.

32. After graduating from middle school, his mother took him to Europe.

33. Bored and tired, the lecture went over my head.

34. After playing Frisbee all evening, my English paper did not get finished.

35. Crawling across the dusty road I saw a furry little caterpillar.

Key to Practice Quiz on Dangling and Misplaced Modifiers

Rearrange parts of the sentence or rewrite it to eliminate dangling or misplaced modifiers. Other corrections may be possible.

1. After I cleared off the table and put the dishes away, the dog was let into the kitchen. OR After I cleared off the table and put the dishes away, I let the cat into the kitchen.

2. While Stephanie was looking at the store window, her purse was snatched.

3. I tried to wake my sister from her nightmare because she was thrashing about.

4. After getting out of the car and walking up the front steps to my house, I was greeted by my dog at the door.

5. I gave the movie that I didn't like too much to a friend.

6. After I took the test, the professor informed me that I failed.

7. I watched my baby niece, Alison, crawling across the carpet yesterday.

8. Matt and I laughed at the squirrels climbing from tree to tree.

9. After we stood in line for five hours, the manager announced that all tickets were sold.

10. Having broken his hand, he was told by the nurse that he could not play basketball.

11. I will leave the money that you can put in your pocket on the dresser. (This sentence would be best if it were entirely rewritten, such as 'I will put some money on the dresser, and you can put it in your pocket.')

12. When I was nine years old, my father had another child.

13. While Colton was playing soccer, his peanut butter sandwich was stolen.

14. Because she is a funny speaker, I always attended her shows.

15. I gazed at the stars twinkling in the night sky.

16. After I washed and waxed the floor, my dog slid across the room.

17. When I was at the age of seven, my parents bought a new house.

18. I am going on a date with a guy named Kade; he owns a scooter.

19. I saw a kite flying through the air.

20. After I finished a week's worth of homework, a beer would have been nice.

21. Tori left with a guy with a Mustang convertible; his name was Cruz.

22. I ducked my head from the angry bird diving through the sky.

23. After I studied for two hours, the grammar assignment went slowly.

24. I couldn't stand to be near her because she was being snooty.

25. After I ran three miles, taking a shower seemed like a good idea.

26. As he took her in his arms, the moon hid behind a cloud.

27. As he thoughtfully began to dress, the new blue jeans and clean shirt reminded him that at last he had a job.

28. Working really hard, she finished the term paper in six hours.

29. When I was ten years old, my mother gave me a ring.

30. After asking three or four people, we finally found the right road.

31. After I cleaned my room, my dog wanted to go for a walk.

32. After he graduated from middle school, his mother took him to Europe.

33. Because I was bored and tired, the lecture went over my head.

34. After playing Frisbee all evening, I did not get my English finished.

35. I saw a furry little caterpillar crawling across the dusty road.

Practice Quiz on Parallel Structure

Correct the following sentences by inserting or deleting words or by rewriting the sentence.

1. High blood pressure can be caused by stress, obesity, and not exercising.

2. After getting up, Keith decided to go out for breakfast, check his mail, and he visited his parents.

3. Women are traditionally the ones who cook, clean, and child care is their responsibility.

4. The facilities of the modern airplane are without a doubt more convenient than the first transport planes.

5. Cardeen reads the *New York Times* every day, does the crossword puzzle, and she never has to use the dictionary.

6. Dentists advise brushing the teeth after each meal and to avoid eating too much sugar.

7. Theodore Roosevelt spoke with warmth and in a humorous vein.

8. My father prefers the intricate plays of football to baseball.

9. Hemingway's success as a novelist was as great a tribute to his style as his plots.

10. The latest trend in architecture is toward simplicity of design and how to be more useful.

Key to Practice Quiz on Parallel Structure

Correct the following sentences by inserting or deleting words or by rewriting the sentence. Changes other than these may be correct.

1. High blood pressure can be caused by stress, obesity, and lack of exercise.

2. After getting up, Keith decided to go out for breakfast, check his mail, and visit his parents.

3. Women are traditionally the ones who cook, clean, and care for children.

4. The facilities of the modern airplane are without a doubt more convenient than those of the first transport planes.

5. Cardeen reads the *New York Times* every day and does the crossword puzzle without ever using the dictionary.

6. Dentists advise their patients to brush their teeth after each meal and to avoid eating too much sugar.

7. Theodore Roosevelt spoke with warmth and humor.

8. My father prefers the intricate plays of football to those of baseball.

9. Hemingway's success as a novelist was as great a tribute to his style as to his plots.

10. The latest trend in architecture is toward practicality and simplicity of design.

Practice Quiz #1 on Editing

Edit all **necessary** usage errors. Do **not** make stylistic changes or add optional commas.

1. Janelle promised to limit her speech to 20 minutes. Although, it went on for half an hour.

2. These flowers are for whomever is willing to sign for them.

3. Its a miracal that Trevor has not had a accident, he drives like a maniack.

4. Until Josh entered the monastery he had lived with his parents and 8 siblings in a three bedroom farmhouse near Jackson Minnesota.

5. The slithery salamander disappeared so quick that Dr. Roths camera captured only a hibiscas leaf.

6. The Professors monotonous drone had a sedative affect on his student's.

7. Reading ones history assignments every night, makes taking quizzes much more easy.

8. The brothers signed up for coarses in ecology and economics, because them and there father wanted the famly farm to go organic.

9. Running through the park in May the aroma of honeysuckle blossoms filled the air.

10. If you walk any slower; you will probally miss the bus.

11. Ever since Tony got his snowboard he has wanted to move to Colorado.

12. Would you like to no who he is.

13. Alissa prefered homework to practising her flute.

14. Because Sharie talks with her hands a lot people often tune out what she says, they become absorped in her body language instead.

Key to Practice Quiz #1 on Editing

Edit all **necessary** usage errors. Do **not** make stylistic changes or add optional commas.

1. Janelle promised to limit her speech to twenty minutes although it went on for half an hour.

2. These flowers are for whoever is willing to sign for them.

3. It's a miracle that Trevor has not had an accident; he drives like a maniac.

4. Until Josh entered the monastery, he had lived with his parents and eight siblings in a three bedroom farmhouse near Jackson, Minnesota.

5. The slithery salamander disappeared so quickly that Dr. Roth's camera captured only a hibiscus leaf.

6. The professor's monotonous drone had a sedative effect on his students.

7. Reading one's history assignments every night makes taking quizzes much easier.

8. The brothers signed up for courses in ecology and economics because they and their father wanted the family farm to go organic.

9. As we ran through the park in May, the aroma of honeysuckle blossoms filled the air.

10. If you walk any more slowly, you will probably miss the bus.

11. Ever since Tony got his snowboard, he has wanted to move to Colorado.

12. Would you like to know who he is?

13. Alissa preferred doing homework to practicing her flute.

14. Because Sharie talks with her hands, a lot of people often tune out what she says; they become absorbed in her body language instead.

Practice Quiz #2 on Editing

Make necessary corrections in spelling, apostrophes, commas, agreement, case forms, verb forms, and adjective/adverb forms. Change sentence structure only to correct dangling modifiers or faulty parallelism. In the blank before each sentence, write S or C to indicate whether the underlined corrected sentence is simple or compound. If there is a blank at the end of the line, write the abbreviation for the italicized pronoun as it functions in the sentence: sub., pn, do, io, op, NPi, or NPg.

_____ 1. Being a teacher, Kathryns weekends were usually spent grading papers and she choose the relative solitude of her cabin up north for this activety.

_____ 2. On Saturday night she was sitting at the kichen table having a cup on chai latte and was reading essays.

_____ 3. In the quite of the house a sound from the cold air register disterbed her consentration.

_____ 4. At first she imagines that it is a mouse, then she realized that was only wishful thinking.

_____ 5. Because it had to be a bat.

_____ 6. Bats never bothered Kathryn outside but in the house *they* sent *her* into hysterics.
_____ _____

_____ 7. *She* having to deal with this flying rodent gave *her* the shakes. _____ _____

_____ 8. Her first thought was to simply go to a motel, however the bat would still be their in the morning.

_____ 9. Her next thought was this: it would be better for *her* to have to smell a dead bat in the duct work then for *her* to wait in terror for it to crawl out of the vent. _____

_____ 10. She piled books and magazines on top of the cold air register's in the floor.

_____ 11. Most of the hot air register's had greats with openings much more small than a bat so *they* did not worry *her*. _____ _____

_____ 12. Two of *them* however, needed to be covered. _____

_____ 13. Kneeling down by the register and trying to tape a paper bag over the openings the bat suddenly flies right up behind *her*. _____

_____ 14. Uncharacteristicly *she* let out a string of epithets and fled the cabin. _____

_____ 15. Standing in the cold with the door wide open Kathryn suddenly remembered the bath tub.

_____ 16. It was steadily filling up with water for her nightly relaxing soak.

_____ 17. How long would it take for that bat to find the open doorway and allow *her* to go back inside. _____

Key to Practice Quiz #2 on Editing

Make necessary corrections in spelling, apostrophes, commas, agreement, case forms, verb forms, and adjective/adverb forms. Change sentence structure only to correct dangling modifiers or faulty parallelism. In the blank before each sentence, write S, C, CX, or CCX to indicate whether the <u>corrected</u> sentence is simple, compound, complex, or compound-complex. If there is a blank at the end of the line, write the abbreviation for the italicized pronoun as it functions in the sentence: sub., pn, do, io, op, NPi, or NPg.

<u>CCX</u> 1. Because Kathryn was a teacher, her weekends were usually spent grading papers, and she chose the relative solitude of her cabin up north for this activity.

<u>S</u> 2. On Saturday night she was sitting at the kitchen table having a cup of chai latte and reading essays.

<u>S</u> 3. In the quiet of the house, a sound from the cold air register disturbed her concentration.

<u>CCX</u> 4. At first she imagined that it was a mouse; then she realized that this was only wishful thinking.

<u>S</u> 5. It had to be a bat.

<u>C</u> 6. Bats never bothered Kathryn outside, but in the house *they* sent *her* into hysterics.

<u>sub</u>   <u>do</u>

<u>S</u> 7. *Her* having to deal with this flying rodent gave *her* the shakes. <u>NPg</u> <u>io</u>

<u>C</u> 8. Her first thought was to simply go to a motel; however, the bat would still be there in the morning.

<u>C</u> 9. Her next thought was this: it would be better for her to have to smell a dead bat in the duct work than for *her* to wait in terror for it to crawl out of the vent. <u>NPi</u>

<u>S</u> 10. She piled books and magazines on top of the cold air registers in the floor.

<u>C</u> 11. Most of the hot air registers had grates with openings much smaller than a bat, so *they* did not worry *her*. <u>sub</u>   <u>do</u>

<u>S</u> 12. Two of *them,* however, needed to be covered. <u>op</u>

<u>CX</u> 13. As she knelt down by the register and tried to tape a paper bag over the openings, the bat suddenly flew right up behind *her*. <u>op</u>

<u>S</u> 14. Uncharacteristically *she* let out a string of epithets and fled the cabin. <u>sub</u>

S 15. Standing in the cold with the door wide open, Kathryn suddenly remembered the bath tub.

 S 16. It was steadily filling up with water for her nightly, relaxing soak.

 S 17. How long would it take for that bat to find the open doorway and allow *her* to go back inside? NPi

Practice Quiz #3 on Editing

Correct the errors in spelling, punctuation, agreement, case, verb forms, modifiers, and parallelism. Do not change capitalization or periods.

Between Jean, Jim, and I, Jim felt the affects of our parents divorce more. He could of went to college right after high school but desided to sell insurance insted. At first he made alot of money however him and his freinds had expensive recreationel activitys such as, beting on race cars. Just between you and me, I though he would never settle down. When he met Tami however he begun to change. For someone whom had staid out late every night I was glad to see him becoming quite domestic. No matter who I talked to, they would all say Whats going on with you're brother. We hardly never see him any more.

Him and Tami use to spend there evenings reading, watching TV, and they would talk about the future. It was apparant to both he and she that living ment growing. Jim had always liked electronics and he decided too persue his intrest by enroling in a class at the local technical college. Since Mr. Goodwin his high school principle lived near by Jim first asked him weather he thought it was a good idea. Mr. Goodwins reply was That's an absolute excellent step foreward. Ill right a recommendation letter for you. That was three years ago. Jim is now working for a large trucking firm on its information technology team. He says that going to college was the best thing he ever did and that meeting Tami was the luckiest.

Key to Practice Quiz #3 on Editing

Correct the errors in spelling, punctuation, agreement, case, verb forms, modifiers, and parallelism. Do not change capitalization or periods.

Among Jean, Jim, and I, Jim felt the effects of our parents' divorce most. He could have gone to college right after high school but decided to sell insurance instead. At first he made a lot of money; however, he and his friends had expensive recreational activities, such as betting on race cars. Just between you and me, I thought he would never settle down. When he met Tami, however, he began to change. For someone who had stayed out late every night, he was becoming quite domestic. No matter whom I talked to, they would all say, "What's going on with your brother? We hardly ever see him anymore.

He and Tami used to spend their evenings reading, watching TV, and talking about the future. It was apparent to both him and her that living meant growing. Jim had always liked electronics, and he decided to pursue his interest by enrolling in a class at the local technical college. Since Mr. Goodwin, his high school principal, lived nearby, Jim first asked him whether he thought it was a good idea. Mr. Goodwin's reply was, "That's an absolutely excellent step forward. I'll write a recommendation letter for you." That was three years ago. Jim is now working for a large trucking firm on its information technology team. He says that going to college was the best thing he ever did and that meeting Tami was the luckiest.

Practice Quiz #4 on Editing

Correct spelling, punctuation, agreement, dangling or misplaced modifiers, adjective/adverb use and faulty parallelism. In the blanks after the sentences, indicate how each italicized pronoun functions in its clause: **sub** (subject), **pn** (predicate noun), **do** (direct object), **io** (indirect object), **op** (object of preposition), **NPi** (noun phrase "subject" of infinitive), or **NPg** (noun phrase "subject" of gerund). In the blank at the beginning of the corrected sentence, write **S** if it is simple, **C** if it is compound, **CX** if it is complex, and **CCX** if it is compound-complex. Do not change capitalization.

____ 1. James is the person *whom* I have looked up to since I was a child. _____

____ 2. Drive slow, theres alot of deer in this area.

____ 3. Lifting with your legs instead of your back, that box will not feel so heavily.

____ 4. Neither Bill nor his friends likes to bowl however every one of *them* are real enthused about outdoor sports. _____

____ 5. After runing for presidant of the nature society all of the members congradulated Kena on her vicory.

____ 6. Why does youre dog behave so bad.

____ 7. Under the circumstanses *he* should of went to technical college instead of the university. _____

____ 8. As the sun rose the bus driver pulled a tinted sheet of plastic over his windsheild so that *he* could see easier. _____

____ 9. Am *I* the person *who* you wanted to ask about the busses to the game. _____ _____

____ 10. Everyone should bring their own bevrages to the party which will start at 8:00.

____ 11. While finishing her seventeenth centry poctry test Bobbi acquired a massive headache and left the room to get some water to wash down her migrain pills.

____ 12. Can I give this to *whoever* wants it. _____

____ 13. Whether permiting *we* plan to play eighteen holes of golf tomorrow and eighteen the next day. _____

____ 14. Anybody *who* you chose for the parts in the play are bound to do real good.

_____

____ 15. Because she was convinsed that marrage would cramp her style Jana turned down Kyles proposel so he decided to look for someone *who* was interested in raising a family. _____

Key to Practice Quiz #4 on Editing

Correct spelling, punctuation, agreement, dangling or misplaced modifiers, adjective/adverb use and faulty parallelism. In the blanks after the sentences, indicate how each italicized pronoun functions in its clause: **sub** (subject), **pn** (predicate noun), **do** (direct object), **io** (indirect object), **op** (object of preposition), **NPi** (noun phrase "subject" of infinitive), or **NPg** (noun phrase "subject" of gerund). In the blank at the beginning of the <u>corrected</u> sentence, write **S** if it is simple, **C** if it is compound, **CX** if it is complex, and **CCX** if it is compound-complex. <u>Do not change capitalization.</u>

_CX_ 1. James is the person *whom* I have looked up to since I was a child. _op_

_C_ 2. Drive slowly; there are a lot of deer in this area.

_CX_ 3. If you lift with your legs instead of your back, that box will not feel so heavy.

_C_ 4. Neither Bill nor his friends like to bowl; however, every one of *them* is really enthusiastic about outdoor sports. _op_

_CX_ 5. After Kena ran for president of the nature society, all of the members congratulated her on her victory.

_S_ 6. Why does your dog behave so badly?

_S_ 7. Under the circumstances *he* should have gone to technical college instead of the university. _sub_

_CX_ 8. As the sun rose, the bus driver pulled a tinted sheet of plastic over his windshield so that *he* could see more easily. _sub_

_CX_ 9. Am *I* the person *whom* you wanted to ask about the buses to the game?
     sub _do_

207

_CX_ 10. Everyone should bring his or her own beverages to the party, which will start at

8:00.

_S_ 11. While finishing her seventeenth century poetry test, Bobbi acquired a massive

headache and left the room to get some water to wash down her migraine pills.

_CX_ 12. Can I give this to *whoever* wants it? _sub_

_S_ 13. Weather permitting, *we* plan to play eighteen holes of golf tomorrow and

eighteen the next day. _sub_

_CX_ 14. Anybody *whom* you chose for the parts in the play is bound to do really well.

_do_

CCX 15. Because she was convinced that marriage would cramp her style, Jana

turned down Kyle's proposal; so he decided to look for someone *who* was interested in

raising a family. _sub_

Practice Quiz #5 on Editing

Make all necessary corrections in usage.

1. Looking across the beach, a wave crashed against the shore.

2. My 12 year-old dog Gorda has grown taller then me.

3. I choose to get advise from my sister when we were shoping for cloths.

4. She was going on a date with a guy who owned 2 houses named Bob.

5. That coment was the most perfect complement she had ever recieved although she was not expectting to hear it from him so quick.

6. Each of the women has their own special nack for getting their children to do their homework.

7. The snow and temperature are the reason Alice dose not want to go outside.

8. My conscious would not let me charge my personnel expenses to my busness expense account.

9. There are less mistakes then I thought.

10. He was born in Chicago Illinois on July 7 1982.

11. After finishing our English homework, the pizza tasted great.

12. This is just between you and I.

13. You should always give a child constructive feedback on their work, so they can improve.

14. I am going to the store, buying a watermelon, and I'll cut it at home.

15. The book, The Color Purple focuses on a women developping independance and understanding.

Key to Practice Quiz #5 on Editing

Make all necessary corrections in usage.

1. As we looked across the beach, a wave crashed against the shore.

2. My twelve-year-old dog, Gorda, has grown taller than me.

3. I chose to get advice from my sister when we were shopping for clothes.

4. She was going on a date with a guy named Bob, who owned two houses.

5. That comment was the best compliment she had ever received although she was not expecting to hear it from him so quickly.

6. Each of the women has her own special knack for getting her children to do their homework.

7. The snow and temperature are the reasons Alice does not want to go outside.

8. My conscience would not let me charge my personal expenses to my business expense account.

9. There are fewer mistakes than I thought.

10. He was born in Chicago, Illinois, on July 7, 1982.

11. After we finished our English homework, the pizza tasted great.

12. This is just between you and me.

13. You should always give children constructive feedback on their work so that they can improve.

14. I am going to the store to buy a watermelon, and I'll cut it at home.
    I am going to the store and buying a watermelon; I'll cut it at home.

15. The book *The Color Purple* focuses on a woman developing independence and understanding.

Made in the USA
San Bernardino, CA
01 July 2019